Exquisite Beaded Jewelry

Use Basic Techniques to Create Distinctive Designs

Lynda S. Musante

Published by

An imprint of F+W Publications, Inc.

700 East State Street • Iola, WI 54990-0001
715-445-2214 • 888-457-2873
www.krause.com

Our toll-free number to place an order or obtain a free catalog is (800) 258-0929.

Library of Congress Catalog Number: 2004103293

ISBN: 0-87349-808-9

Edited by Maria L. Turner

Designed by Jamie Griffin

Printed in the United States of America

Dedication

For Lou, Laurel, and Robbie, who have supported my creative efforts throughout the years and still don't mind going to the bead store in every town we visit.

Acknowledgments

I sincerely appreciate the guidance and leadership from my editor, Maria Turner. Her expert eye and patience were invaluable for the completion of this book.

I'd also like to thank photographer Kris Kandler for her suggestions and quiet expertise in the photography of this book, page designer Jamie Griffin for making the pages come to life, and cover designer Mary Lou Marshall for a simply "exquisite" look.

Julie Stephani, my acquisition editor, you're a dear friend, and it was so nice to work with you after all these years.

I'd further like to thank the contributing artists who sent in amazing work for this book, as well as the manufacturers who generously supplied product for my design work.

Table of Contents

Introduction

Since the earliest recorded time, stone, bone, clay, and shells have been strung and worn as adornment. In early times, beadwork often defined a culture and its wealth. In this book, let's define beading as the act of assembling beads into a wearable decorative embellishment. Beads can be stitched, woven, wired, glued, or embedded. It's the influence and experiences of the artist that transforms these—often tiny, sometimes large—beads into a work of art.

One aspect that makes beading so attractive is that the artist can explore and combine the same materials and achieve many different results, through the influences of technique and composition.

The availability of beads and materials in shops, shows, and on Web sites also make this art more accessible. Finding beads from most every culture is infinitely easier today than ever before. The Internet has widened the availability for finding beads—both the lampwork variety and the semiprecious stones.

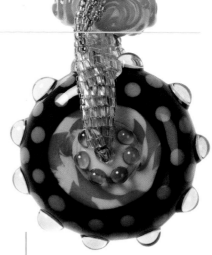

Focal bead by Ellie Mac.

For me, most of the pieces start off with a loose idea of the bead colors, textures, techniques, and any other materials. Once I begin working, the beads will seem to lead me in one direction or another through how they are going together and what beads I seem to be focused on using. In this book, this process is defined as "improvisational beadwork." Projects completed using this method often look more organic, and more often, they are the projects I enjoy the most once they are completed.

The old adage, "a picture is worth a thousand words," certainly rings true for beadwork. Throughout the chapters, there are many close-up photographs of the gallery artists' work. The goal for these insets is to give you the opportunity to examine the composition and construction of the beadwork. The intricacy of the workmanship is often innovative, inspiring, and intriguing.

I hope to help you build and expand your skills; find your own voice in your beadwork—to discover your "look"; and, perhaps, challenge you to look at your beadwork differently. There are so many variations, techniques, and possibilities found in beadwork, that you could work with the same combination of beads and never make the same project twice. As you become more proficient, I hope you'll begin to experiment, to work with new colors or new textures, and to create pieces that reflect you.

Lynda Musante

Improvisational beadwork featuring lampwork beads by Kristan Childs, Redside Designs.

I've created with my hands just about all my life. I enjoy experimenting and the discovery of trying out new materials and techniques. I am a self-taught beader for the most part. I love the portability of working with beads, and the ability to work just about anywhere there's a good light. With this in mind, all of the projects in this book are created using basic, readily available hand-tools, beads, and materials.

Bracelet created with wire, seed beads, and lampwork beads by Kristan Childs, Redside Designs.

CHAPTER I

As you Begin

Learning the basics is the best way to start any new type of craft. In this chapter, you will find many questions to help jumpstart your thought process in deciding what you want to make. Relax and let the creativity begin!

Comfort, Considerations, and Inspiration

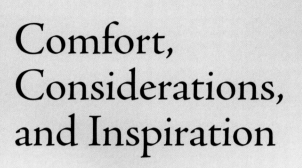

Making your own jewelry is a wonderful way to express yourself creatively, to make gifts for friends and family, or even as part of a home-based business. Jewelry-making can be a very satisfying, portable means of self-expression.

The wonderful thing about making your own jewelry is the ability you'll develop to put your own imprint onto the pieces you make. The fun of creating exquisite jewelry can be found in the sense of satisfaction when the piece turns out as you imagined it would. Compliments of friends, family, and even strangers will build your confidence and feelings of accomplishment.

Use this book as a tool to look at jewelry-making in a new way. While there are many projects to try out in this book, you won't find much in the way of bead-by-bead instructions or charts for exactly replicating the jewelry found here. I believe it's important for you to find you own voice, to create your own

Strung necklace with drilled and embellished domino as pendant.

look. I hope you'll consider this book to be a resource you'll turn to again and again for inspiration or explanation of a technique. What you will find are exercises to stretch your thought process and insights into how to approach creating projects.

Each chapter outlines, explains, and contains a variety of projects to build your skills in jewelry-making from basic identification of beads through construction of projects that combine stringing, wirework, and improvisational stitching. Each of the skill-building chapters also contains a gallery section of pieces by sensational bead artists that showcase the techniques explored in the chapter.

Learning Problem-Solving Techniques

Once you master the basic skills in jewelry making, you'll build the confidence you need to experiment and lose the fear of beginning a project without a known outcome. Learning

problem-solving techniques is essential to developing your skills. Sometimes you just have to cut something up and use the parts in another project.

So, What Do You Want to Make?

Think about what kind of jewelry you like to wear. Look in your jewelry box. What do you see? Do you prefer long, dangling earrings or studs? Delicate, small necklaces or bold statement pieces? Do you like thin bangles or wide cuffs?

What materials attract your attention? What techniques appeal to you? Stitching? Stringing? Do a combination of techniques and materials pique your interest? Do you like traditional pieces that are balanced and symmetrical? Does the abstract interest you?

So, where do you find inspiration? Look through books to expand your knowledge of techniques. Look at the jewelry you see in magazine advertisements. Look at the jewelry that celebrities wear on your favorite shows. Window-shop at the mall, at galleries and in artist co-ops. Surf the Internet and read about what other jewelry designers are doing. Check out the Web sites of successful jewelry businesses. Examine mail-order catalogs. Attend shows or take classes. Keeping a file of photos that appeal to you is extremely helpful in developing projects.

Comfortable Jewelry

Jewelry that is designed to fit the wearer is a pleasure to wear. As you are creating your jewelry, be sure to stop frequently and try on the piece, see how it fits, how it looks on you, and how it is meeting your vision of what you want it to be when it's complete. Ask yourself the following questions:

- How does it fit? Does it need to be larger or smaller?

- Is it smooth? Does it need more texture?

- Are you being poked? Should you file wire or trim the ends of the stringing material closer?

- Is the piece in proportion? Should it be wider or longer? Perhaps it should be smaller and more delicate?

- If you're creating a necklace, does it feel balanced on the neck? If not, do you need a counterbalance? Perhaps a modification in the piece will allow it to be worn more comfortably?

Simple peyote-stitched fold-over earrings.

Tip:

Your comfort while making jewelry is important, too. Creating jewelry requires the artist to hold the artwork and tools, to exert pressure on the materials, and to perform repetitive motions ... sometimes for hours at a time. Here's how to make it more enjoyable:

- Sit in a comfortable chair with good back support. Have a footstool nearby to be able to elevate your legs once in a while.

- Be sure to have good light to work in. Today, there are many lights available that are adjustable in height and come with bulbs that are color-correcting, so if you work at night, you will be able to see the actual colors of your beads and how they appear together.

- Be sure to stop frequently and roll your head around on your neck in both directions, stretch your arms and shoulders, and flex your hands up and down. The more you stop and stretch the muscles in your neck, back, and arms, the easier it will be to work on your jewelry for long periods.

A Few Thoughts for Success

Think about the "wearability" of what you're creating. Developing a piece with several glass focal beads may make for an incredible-looking piece of jewelry, but will the weight of all that glass make the piece uncomfortable to wear for any period of time? I can't stress it enough: When creating jewelry, be sure to keep the wearer in mind. If a piece of jewelry is uncomfortable, it won't be worn.

Keep in mind that you may need to remake something two, three, or more times until the project is finished. Causes for remaking a project might include the following: the length (too long or too short); proportion; balance; comfort; or value. Remember though, every time you remake something, you will build on your skills as you go. So, the time spent on reworking something is not lost.

Be sure to record your bead purchases, their value, and where they were purchased. When planning projects, it's helpful to have an inventory of the beads you have on hand and to know where to go to get additional beads if you're short of a particular style or color. If you maintain good records, and eventually begin to sell your finished jewelry, you will need to know how to assign a value to your projects.

Also, make it a practice to photograph your completed projects. Take close-up images as well, so you can see any special innovations you may have included in a project. If you regularly give away your jewelry as gifts, it's helpful to have a record of what you've completed.

Frequently review your photos to see how you've developed in your techniques and abilities. You'll be able to see if you have a particular affinity for a certain style, technique, or color combination in your work. Being able to review your body of work is a nice opportunity to evaluate your growth and talents as they've developed over time.

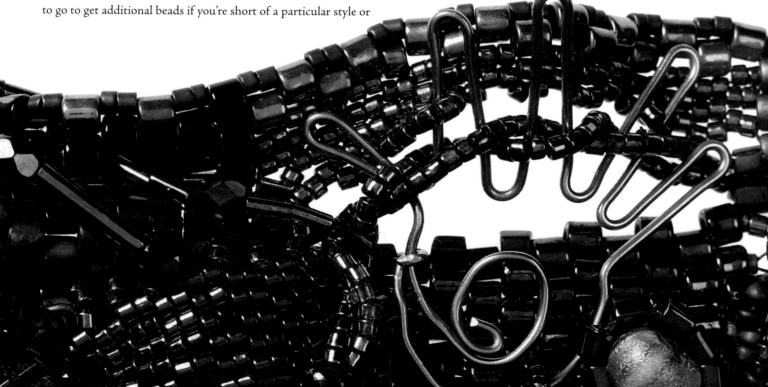

CHAPTER 2

IT'S ALL ABOUT THE BEADS

Many new beaders sometimes find it difficult to commit their bead purchases to a project. I think everyone goes through a hoarding period when starting out. Once you are ready, sometimes bead projects featuring hoarded beads will pop into your head, while other times, you can be inspired by another artist's piece. Then, you'll be ready to commit the beads to a project and get going.

This multi-strand tourmaline necklace is choker length with uniform strand lengths and features a focal bead by glass artist Karen Ovington.

Size Considerations

Proportion is extremely important when creating jewelry. Two general considerations are the overall body size of the wearer and the wearer's bosom size.

The first consideration will help you determine the size of piece necessary to be in proportion to the wearer. A very petite person would be overwhelmed and uncomfortable with a large-scale piece and would find a delicate piece more appropriate. A larger person can wear larger pieces without the loss of scale.

For the second consideration, the bosom size affects how a necklace hangs when worn, and in many cases, dictates how long a necklace should be overall.

Grouping containers of seed beads and focal beads helps in selecting colors for a project.

Planning Makes Projects Easier at First

In addition to the length of your project, you should start considering other key design elements. By considering the following in the development phase, you can begin to plan the look of your piece before you begin assembling the components.

Balance

Will the piece be symmetrical? Symmetrical pieces are a mirror image on the left and right sides. Asymmetrical pieces can be extremely interesting, but will involve some challenges in design. Creating a piece that contains asymmetrically sized beads may require designing in a counterbalance bead to hang from the clasp, as this will prevent the weight of the larger, asymmetrical beads from causing the necklace to slide around while being worn.

Texture

Will your piece have a lot of dimension? Open spaces? Texture can be introduced with the materials themselves—using branched coral beads, for example—or with technique, by creating branched fringe.

Color

What colors will be included in your project? Some designers plan out a color theme to their piece before they ever start selecting materials. Others choose their focal beads and build their bead color selections based on those beads.

Gather the beads you want to use in a project and place them onto a white surface (could be a piece of paper). In natural light, squint slightly and look at the beads. Ask yourself the following questions:

- What color seems to be the most prominent? Is this the color you want the project to feature?

- What color seems to disappear?

- Do the colors seem to be compatible? Or, if harmony is not your goal, does the contrast seem to fit your concept?

- Do the materials gathered complement each other? If you're using high-quality materials, does the style of the clasp complement the quality of the beads? If you're using rustic clay pieces, do they complement the other beads and findings?

This detail photo of an amulet bag shows texture created by the addition of wire, bugle beads, and varying styles and sizes of seed beads.

Determining the Elements

Almost every piece of jewelry can be broken down into the following components.

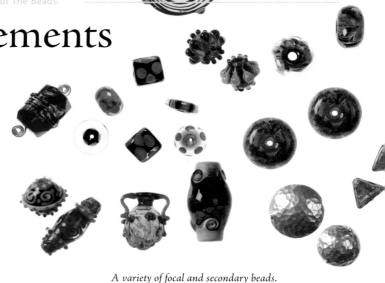

A variety of focal and secondary beads.

Focal Beads

These are the beads that are the focus of the piece and are often located at the center and front of a necklace. Often, these beads determine the colors and sizes of the other beads in the project. These are the "look at me!" eye candy of the piece.

Be sure to consider how you will attach your focal bead. Is the hole large enough to accommodate the materials you want to string or stitch through it? Or, if there is an extremely large hole through the center of the bead, how will it be attached? Thinking these issues through in the beginning will make the assembly process smoother.

Secondary Beads

These beads are smaller and less showy than the focal beads. They are often distributed throughout the piece for visual continuity. These beads are typically placed near the front and sides of a piece so they are viewed when the piece is worn. These beads can be selected to complement the focal bead(s) or to contribute additional color or texture to a project.

Filler Beads

These are seed beads and/or very small beads used to tie the focal and secondary beads together. Frequently, filler beads can be the focus of a necklace when they are stitched together into a larger piece, as in sculptural or freeform peyote-stitched pieces.

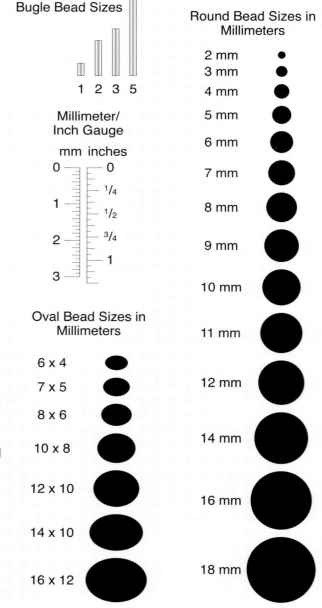

Beads are traditionally measured using the metric system, and the chart below shows many of the common sizes of beads available today.

Seed Beads Per Inch

Use these approximate counts of seed beads per inch to help plan your own designs.

Bead Size	Beads per inch
11°	20
8°	12
5°	7

Many of today's popular bead shapes used in creating jewelry

Bead Shapes

Beads are manufactured in a variety of shapes and to order beads online or in a store it is helpful to know how to refer to the beads you need. Many of the names are very commonsensical. There are exceptions to every style, but for the most part the following descriptions are accurate:

Bugles are long, thin, and tube-shaped, and available in a variety of lengths and finishes. Bugles can be smooth or twisted.

Barrels are cylindrical, but slightly rounded around the center, and flat on both ends.

Bicones are larger in the center and tapered at both ends, often faceted and made of crystal.

Briolettes are purse-shaped with a hole drilled horizontally through the top. They are often created from semiprecious stones and can be faceted to catch the light.

Cubes are square, sometimes with facets cut on the edges, with a hole that can go through the flat sides or diagonally, from corner to corner.

Disks are usually flat and round, shaped like a coin that is often somewhat rounded in the center of the disk. The hole is usually through the center of the flat sides, but can be drilled from edge to edge.

Faceted beads contain many flat surfaces that catch the light and reflect it. Faceted beads are found in a wide variety of shapes, such as round, teardrop, and barrel. They are often treated with a variety of finishes that help reflect the light.

Heishi beads are very small, irregular disks, usually metal and used in multiples.

Hexagonals are six-sided with either tapered or blunt ends. Often, hexagonal beads are also faceted to reflect light or are treated with finishes.

Ovals are similar in shape to the barrel bead, though more rounded through the "hip" area. Oval beads usually are drilled from end to end.

Pressed are made of glass or clay and shaped by a mold to form a recognizable figure like a flower or leaf. Many glass beads from Czechoslovakia are pressed glass.

Tabular beads are flat, as if it were a round oval bead that was flattened under a weight, and is most frequently drilled from end to end.

Triangular beads are flat with a triangular shape and the hole running from the point to the opposite side, or in seed beads, they are triangular, appearing to be cut from a hollow triangular rod.

Seed beads are tiny and round with the hole drilled in the center. Seed beads come in various sizes, shapes, colors, and finishes, and are the most widely used bead in jewelry making, as detailed in the Seed Bead section, page 17.

Bead set created by Dorris Sorensen.

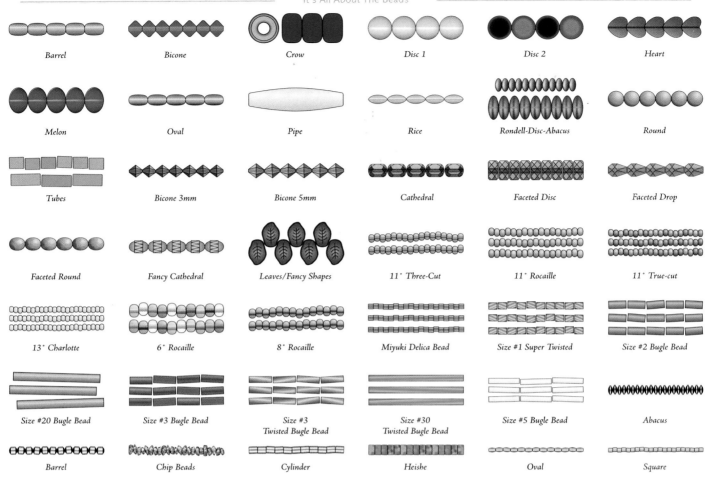

Barrel

Bicone

Crow

Disc 1

Disc 2

Heart

Melon

Oval

Pipe

Rice

Rondell-Disc-Abacus

Round

Tubes

Bicone 3mm

Bicone 5mm

Cathedral

Faceted Disc

Faceted Drop

Faceted Round

Fancy Cathedral

Leaves/Fancy Shapes

11˚ Three-Cut

11˚ Rocaille

11˚ True-cut

13˚ Charlotte

6˚ Rocaille

8˚ Rocaille

Miyuki Delica Bead

Size #1 Super Twisted

Size #2 Bugle Bead

Size #20 Bugle Bead

Size #3 Bugle Bead

Size #3
Twisted Bugle Bead

Size #30
Twisted Bugle Bead

Size #5 Bugle Bead

Abacus

Barrel

Chip Beads

Cylinder

Heishe

Oval

Square

United by color theme, these glass beads have a variety of shapes.

The influence of other cultures is widely found in much of the beadwork created today. In the accompanying photo, you'll see red Cinnabar, cloisonné, ceramic, Balinese silver, Peruvian silver, African glass, blue-green Egyptian faience, Greek metal, and Czechoslovakian glass beads.

Beads from around the world.

16

Seed Beads

This ceramic watercolor dish contains beads in varying sizes and finishes.

The category of beads referred to as seed beads include the smallest and most plentiful beads used in creating jewelry. The techniques used in seed bead manufacturing are ancient. There's evidence that beads were created in many different regions of the world.

In Japan, seed beads are machine-made and tend to be very consistent in size and shape. Japanese seed beads are very desirable for stitched bead projects that require the needle and beading thread to pass through a number of times as the piece is worked.

Traditionally, seed beads are measured in increments called "aughts" (with aught = 0). The larger the number assigned to a bead, the smaller the bead is in size. For example, 11/0 beads are larger than 15/0 beads, but smaller than 6/0 beads.

Culling your beads refers to the process of pouring the beads into a flat dish and sorting through them to remove beads that are odd-sized, have sharp edges, or are poorly formed. If you are creating a project with peyote stitch, the irregularity in the beads will be very noticeable. Of all the beads, bugle beads definitely need to be culled, as their sharp ends may cut your thread once the piece is completed.

The beads on the bottom have been etched, while those on the top are not. Lampwork beads by Kim Ballor.

Bead Finishes

The finish of the beads, particularly on seed beads, greatly affects the appearance of your project. The following is a partial list of the popular finishes available on seed beads:

- Aurora borealis (iridescent)
- Fire-polished (looks like the reflection of oil floating on water)
- Galvanized (finish is likely to rub off, so keep that in mind when using and placing these beads on a project)
- Matte
- Metallic
- Miracle beads (have a clear glass coating that refracts the light and intensifies the color)
- Opaque
- Silver-lined
- Sparkling
- Semi-matte
- Transparent

The degree of transparency of the beads can add more design possibilities, as using a colored thread can influence the final appearance of the beads.

Changing a Bead's Appearance

You can easily modify the finish of your beads by soaking them in an etching solution. I've discovered that some inexpensive seed beads take on a more rich and expensive appearance when etched. Also, consider etching your beads when combining beads that may have slightly different finishes, as this will unify the appearance of your project.

Be sure to conduct a small test batch before putting all your beads into the etching solution and be sure to follow the manufacturer's safety instructions.

Specialty Beads

There are such a variety of focal beads, that those shown here are just a small sampling of the variety of beads available for use in jewelry creation.

Crown beads by Nancy Pilgrim.

Focal bead by Doug Remschneider.

Focal beads by Kennebunkport Beads.

"Fritter" bead by Heart Bead Art Glass.

Lampwork

A glass artist creates artist lampwork beads one at a time in a torch. These beads should be annealed (gradually and carefully cooled) for strength and durability. When purchasing lampwork beads, ask about the annealing process, since beads that are poorly annealed will crack and break when worn or bumped against a hard surface.

The cost of lampwork beads is influenced by the complexity and time required to create them.

Often, lampwork artists will explore a particular glass technique and create coordinating sets of beads. These beads can be used as either focal or secondary beads, depending on the type of project you're developing.

Some artists develop themes when creating lampwork beads.

Pate de Verre bead by Donna Milliron.

"Wish" beads by Kim Ballor.

Napa Valley bead by Sharon Peters, Smart Ass Glass.

Urn bead from Blue Heeler Glass.

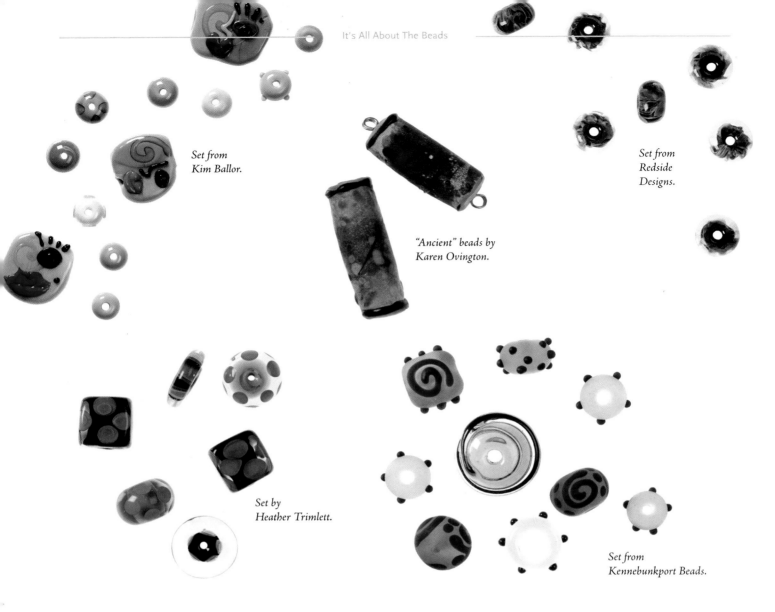

Set from
Kim Ballor.

"Ancient" beads by
Karen Ovington.

Set from
Redside
Designs.

Set by
Heather Trimlett.

Set from
Kennebunkport Beads.

Polymer Clay

Polymer clay is a soft, manufactured clay that can be mixed, blended, and then baked to cure to a hardened state. In the hands of a master artist, polymer clay can be transformed to appear like many other materials, such as semiprecious stone or wood.

Focal bead by
Barbara McGuire.

Precious Metal Clay

PMC is another new revolutionary material that has dramatically influenced the jewelry making community. Microscopic particles of pure silver or pure gold are combined with water and an organic binder, resulting in a material that looks, feels, and can be sculpted like clay. Firing a dried piece of PMC in a kiln burns away the binder and leaves behind a pure silver piece.

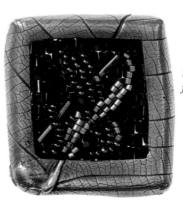

PMC leaf impression
frame by the author.

CHAPTER 3

KNOWING YOUR TOOLS AND MATERIALS

Be sure to purchase the best-quality tools possible when you begin. The better-quality tools are designed to be ergonomic, and the joints are made to withstand use for years of jewelry creation.

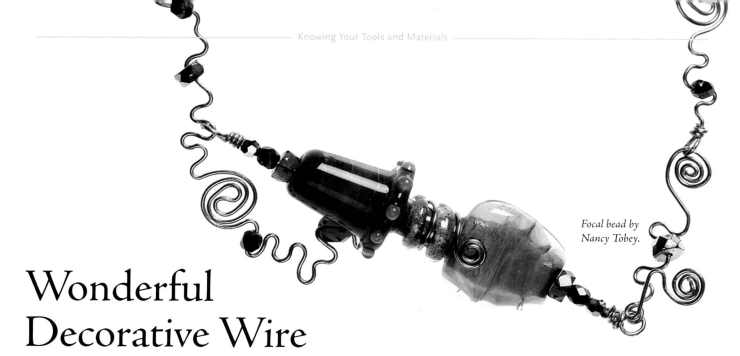

Focal bead by Nancy Tobey.

Wonderful Decorative Wire

The ability to create your own links and jump rings with wire will give your jewelry piece a different look than a project created using purchased findings, links, or jump rings.

As with most any creative endeavor, practice makes perfect. I strongly recommend that you purchase inexpensive copper or brass wire from the hardware store and practice making findings with that material before working with silver or other precious metals. Copper and brass wire are softer metals and easier to bend when learning new techniques. Save the gold, silver and niobium wires for when you're comfortable with the techniques.

Wire Types

There are many types of wire to choose from, so you will want to consider the overall look of your piece when making your selection. Each metal has its own characteristics and considerations.

Gold can be expensive and soft, but it doesn't tarnish. Gold brings warmth to any jewelry piece, while increasing the cost and perceived value.

Silver is less expensive than gold and available in a variety of hardnesses. Silver contributes a cool feeling to a piece. It is considered more valuable than copper or other base metals.

Copper offers a rustic and earthy tone to jewelry. While copper is not considered a high-quality material, often the color of the wire contributes to the overall look of a piece, which outweighs any regard for the material. Copper wire requires hardening to maintain its shape.

Niobium wire is usually available in limited gauges and a few intense, bright colors. The expensive niobium coating is extremely fragile and will crack if not treated carefully. To assist in preventing the damage to coated wires, purchase pliers with coated jaws or wrap the jaws of your tools with masking tape.

A Guide for Selecting Wire

Knowing what gauge and type of wire to use for different applications is helpful in choosing the right wire for your jewelry project. Wire is measured in gauges. The higher the gauge number, the thinner the wire (just like seed beads). For example, 12-gauge wire is much heavier than a typical wire clothes hanger, and 36-gauge wire is thinner than many sewing threads.

Wire Hardness

The hardness of the wire also must be considered in selecting the wire. Consider the end use for the wire. Generally, the harder the wire, the stiffer it will be, which will influence the types of project the wire is used in.

Dead Soft Wire is extremely soft and can be easily bent with pliers and fingers. It is often used in wire wrapping, where wire is wrapped around a large bead or gemstone. Dead soft wire should not be used for earring findings or in other wirework that sustains wear and weight.

Half-Hard Wire has been annealed (heated), and when shaped, will retain the form. It is preferred for creating jewelry findings, clasps, pins, and decorative pieces in jewelry. Half-hard wire can be hardened even further with hammering so it maintains its shape when formed.

Memory Wire is an extremely hard and brittle wire that is generally sold in a spring form. Never cut memory wire with wire cutters, as it is so hard it will damage the blade. To break memory wire, firmly grip the section you wish to break with two chain nose pliers, leaving about a ⅛" gap between the pliers. Flex the pliers back and forth until the memory wire snaps.

Most jewelry findings—like earring wires and clasps—are created using 18- or 20-gauge wire. In making jewelry elements that will withstand the forces of being worn, like a clasp that needs to support the necklace and needs to stay closed, slightly heavier gauges are desirable. The following usages are recommended for half-hard wire:

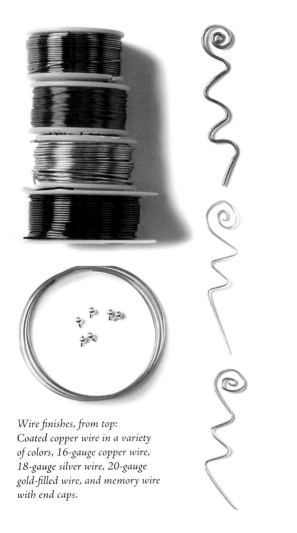

Wire finishes, from top: Coated copper wire in a variety of colors, 16-gauge copper wire, 18-gauge silver wire, 20-gauge gold-filled wire, and memory wire with end caps.

Gauge	Usage
16-gauge	This gauge of wire is too thick and heavy to be used in wire wrapping; however, it can be successfully used to create a variety of decorative elements. Tools are required to form and shape 16-gauge wire, and when manipulated, it will maintain the formed shape without hardening.
18-gauge	A very versatile thickness, 18-gauge wire can be used for clasps, wire wrapping, or forming components with a jewelry jig. This thickness should be work-hardened to maintain shape. Once bent, 18-gauge wire will not completely smooth out. This diameter requires the use of tools, such as a needle nose pliers, to create sharp bends.
20-gauge	This gauge of wire is often used in creating ear wires, attaching beads, wrapping stones, and wrapping found objects. 20-gauge wire should be work-hardened to maintain its shape.
22-gauge	Too lightweight in thickness to use for freeform shaping, ear wires and clasps, it's best to use 22-gauge wire for creating decorative embellishments or attaching light elements to pieces.
24-gauge and thinner	Wires that are 24-gauge and thinner should be used for embellishment and decorative purposes.

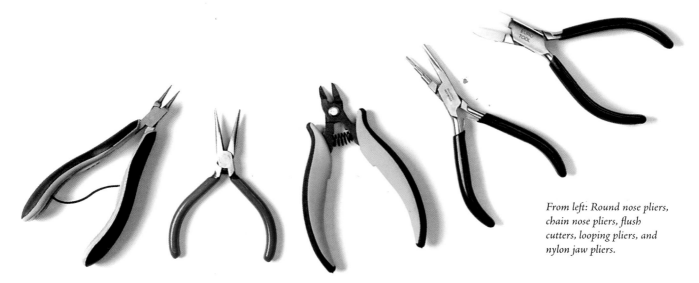

From left: Round nose pliers, chain nose pliers, flush cutters, looping pliers, and nylon jaw pliers.

Wirework Tools

Chain nose pliers have jaws that are flat on the inside and usually rounded on the outside. The flat surface of the jaws allows you to put right-angle bends into the wire. The rounded outside surface allows you to make rounded bends.

Flat nose pliers can also be used for bending wire. These pliers are not rounded on the outside of the jaws.

Flush cutters have angled jaws that allow you to cut off the wire very accurately. When cutting, you'll find that one side of the cut wire will be straight and the other side angled. You may need to have more than one pair of cutters. If you use a variety of wire thicknesses, you will want to have heavy-duty cutters for your thicker wires, like 16-gauge and a lighter-weight pair for your other wires.

Looping pliers have one round and tapered jaw like round nose pliers, but the other side is concave and fits closely to the round side. These pliers are helpful in creating jump rings and coils, as the fit of the jaws assists in bending the wire around the round side.

Nylon jaw pliers have jaws that are molded from nylon. These pliers are used to smooth wire out before use by lightly gripping the wire with the nylon jaws and pulling the wire through. You can also remove unwanted bends in most jewelry weight wires by repeatedly pulling the wire through the nylon jaws after unbending the wire as much as possible with your fingers. This is a valuable tool for beginners, as it enables you to reuse your expensive wire if you do not like how the bends look.

Tip

> When cutting a wire, be sure to hold the cutters away from your face and cover the tool with your other hand. This will prevent any extremely sharp pieces of wire from flying unexpectedly through the air like a champagne cork!

Round nose pliers have rounded jaws, just as the name implies. Use round nose pliers to create loops and curves in wire. Most round nose pliers' jaws taper to a point, which allows you to vary the size of your loops and bends.

Additional Tools

These tools are not used as frequently as the pliers and cutters, but are very effective if you are creating elaborate pieces or making quantities of jewelry.

Bead reamer is a tapered round file that is extremely helpful for opening holes in beads if they are too small for your wire or are irregularly shaped.

Bead reamer.

Flat metal file allows you to file the cut ends of wire. Always, always, always file the cut wire ends as you cut them. It is so much easier to get into this habit as you are learning wirework. Filing the ends of your wires is a sign of good workmanship and attention to detail.

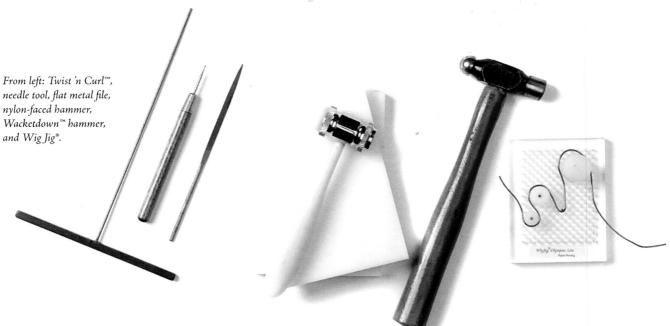

From left: Twist 'n Curl™, needle tool, flat metal file, nylon-faced hammer, Wacketdown™ hammer, and Wig Jig®.

Hammer, like the one shown in the accompanying photo, has a smooth, flat face, as well as a rounded face. Both faces of the hammer can be used to shape and harden wire. Striking the wire with the smooth face of the hammer compresses the wire, causing it to harden. This is how you can ensure your wirework will not pull out of shape while worn. Also, hardening the wire will strengthen a clasp or a curve in an earring finding.

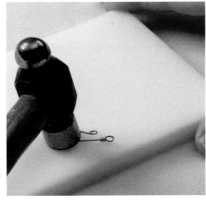

Hammering a hook clasp to work-harden it.

When work-hardening wire, be sure to flip the wire piece so you strike both sides of the piece. If you don't flip the piece while hammering, the wire begins to curve. Further, if your wire piece has places where the wire crosses over itself, cushion the wire piece with a small piece of leather. The leather cushion prevents the wire from becoming too thin and weak from compression in the places it crosses.

Two "S" hook wire clasps; the clasp on the right has been hammered to work-harden it.

Needle tool helps in picking up extremely small beads and in bending metal crimps to round.

Nylon-faced hammer has a replaceable surface that will not mar the finish on the wire. Although more expensive than the metal hammer, this tool offers more versatility in use since the two faces can be used for entirely different effects.

Twist 'n Curl™ is a simple tool that makes coiling wire and creating wire beads extremely easy. The tool consists of a handle and a mandrel with a threaded end. The threaded end is screwed into the handle to anchor it. A hole is located in the handle to anchor the end of your wire. The Twist 'n Curl allows you to save costs and time in making jump rings to coordinate with any jewelry piece, especially if you're using colored wire.

Wacketdown™ can be used as an anvil for hammering wire and will not mar the wire surface. Additionally, you can place a complex-shaped wire piece onto one of the Wacketdown pieces and literally whack it flat with the second piece. This compresses and work-hardens the wire all at one time, and it eliminates the "creeping" that occurs when hammering a wire piece from one end to the other.

Wig Jig® is a tool that allows you to easily reproduce an element again and again. The Wig Jig is a transparent plastic block that has many holes drilled through it, forming a grid pattern. By placing pegs into the holes, you can wind and bend wire around the pegs to create multiples of the same shape, such as earring wires. Because the jig is clear, you also have the option of drawing a pattern on a piece of paper; placing the jig over the pattern; inserting the pegs at the bending points (there are pegs of varying diameters); and shaping your wire.

Wire gauge is a helpful tool in determining the gauge of any wire. The tool has several slots with the gauge indicated beside the slot. To use the wire gauge, you insert the wire into one of the round holes around the edge of the gauge. The hole that most closely fits the wire will have a corresponding number. That number is the wire's gauge.

Wire gauge shown actual size.

Working with Wire

Here is some helpful terminology in working with wire:

Working off the spool means that you should not cut a length of wire before creating a wire element. You will work with the free end of the wire and after bending and shaping the element, cut the wire and file the end smooth.

Working with the wire means that you bend the wire into the direction of the natural curve of the wire, which is most noticeable when you are working off the spool. For example, if creating a spiral, you bend the first curve with the wire, along the curve of the wire.

Working against the wire means you will be bending the wire against the direction of its natural curve.

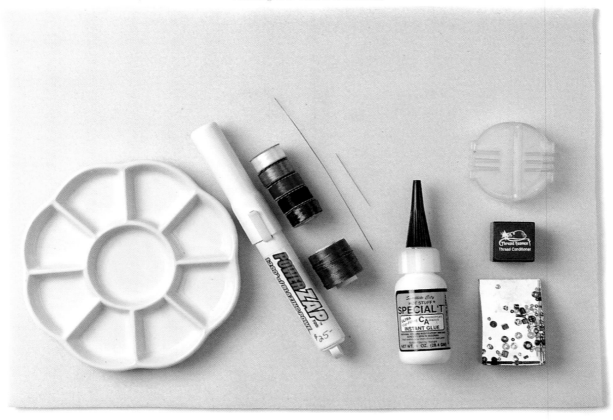

From left: Ceramic watercolor dish; PowerZap; several spools of Nymo thread; Big Eye needle; beading needle; Special-T Glue; beeswax; Thread Heaven; bead scoop; and fleece square.

Stringing Tools

Bead stringing is one of the simplest ways to get started in creating exquisite beaded jewelry. It's amazing how many varied looks you can create by stringing the same beads in different ways. Using good techniques for beginning and ending your strands, as well as using quality materials, ensures that the wearer won't end up with a pile of loose beads.

Beading needles have extremely small and round eyes that are not larger than the diameter of the shaft of the needle so that it can pass through beads easier. The needle size is indicated by a number, and like wire gauges, the larger the number, the smaller the needle size. The most commonly used beading needle sizes are #10 and #12.

Bead scoop is a handy tool for sorting beads back into their original containers.

Beeswax is used to condition threads and will allow the threads to pass easily through small beads. The wax also acts as a lubricant for the threads after you've finished making the project and will extend the wear of the threads used in a piece as it is worn again and again.

To use beeswax, thread your needle and then gently pull the thread across an edge of the beeswax cake. Then, gently pull the thread between your fingers to remove any excess wax. Waxed or conditioned threads tend to tangle less than unconditioned threads.

When threading needles, a longer thread is not always better. You may believe you'll save time in threading the needle less frequently, but you'll more than make up for that time with needing to stop and drop the needle so it unwinds. Also, longer threads tend to tangle up and cause delays when untangling. I usually use a doubled thread when stitching beads together and cut a length that, when doubled, is not quite as long as I can reach when I take a stitch. Threading a needle more frequently is infinitely less frustrating than untangling and unknotting the thread.

Big Eye needle is comprised of two very thin pieces of metal that are welded together at the ends, leaving an eye that is nearly the length of the whole needle in size. These needles are best used on projects without tiny seed beads and that don't require stitching through the beads again and again.

> If you don't have the right size or proper length of needle on hand, you can make your own in a pinch. Take a 6" piece of 26- or 28-gauge wire and fold it in half over your thread. Twist the ends of the wire together and begin to stitch.

Ceramic watercolor dish has deep wells that conveniently hold a variety of beads. The hard surface of the ceramic finish does not allow the needle's tip to pick into it as you scoop your needle through the beads.

Fleece square, when placed on your work area, helps keep your beads from rolling away.

Nymo thread is especially good for beading, as it is slightly waxed and lightly twisted. Nymo is available in several diameters, with each diameter assigned a letter. The thinnest is "A," with diameters continuing to "G." An alternate scale is the use of zeros, with "000" being the thinnest and "0" the thickest. I prefer to use "B" (or "0") for stitched bead projects and "D" for semiprecious or strung projects. Typically, you will purchase your bead thread to closely match your beads so the thread will virtually disappear into your project.

PowerZap can be found in many fishing stores as well as beading stores. The PowerZap consists of an extremely fine wire at the end of a plastic handle. When the power button is pushed, the battery causes the wire to heat up to more than 1,000 degrees. Once heated, you can cut your threads very accurately and close to your beadwork. The PowerZap is also handy for trimming (zapping) any frayed bead threads that may occur as a stitched piece of jewelry is worn for some time. This tool does require good judgment and safe usage practices.

Special-T glue is a quick-drying, flexible glue that dries clear. Special-T glue is compatible with most stringing materials and is an excellent glue for making "illusion" or "tin cup" style necklaces. This glue can also be used for stiffening the ends of thread for stringing or for sealing knots.

Thread Heaven is a synthetic thread conditioner that is used for the same purposes as beeswax.

> Threading a needle can be challenging, especially for older (experienced!) eyes. Make sure you are working in good light. I also wear magnifying glasses when threading needles, just to make it easier to see the tiny eye of the needle. Lightly moisten the end of the thread and grip it with your non-writing hand so that only about ⅛" of thread is showing.
>
> Hold your needle in your writing hand, and bring the needle to the thread and try to put the needle onto the thread. This may seem backwards, but it works! Holding the thread this way supports the end and doesn't allow it to bend as it passes through the eye of the needle.

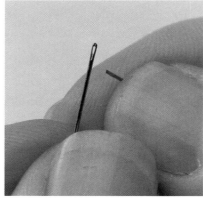

Bringing the eye of the needle to the thread.

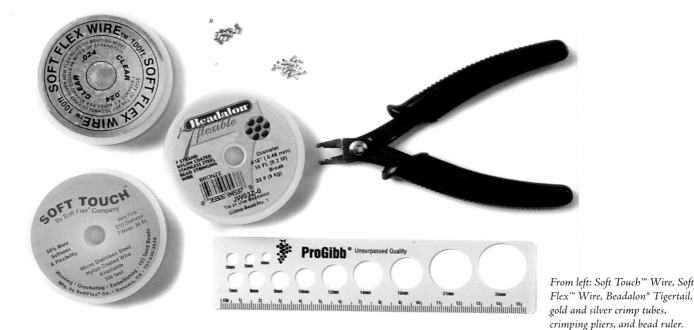

From left: Soft Touch™ Wire, Soft Flex™ Wire, Beadalon® Tigertail, gold and silver crimp tubes, crimping pliers, and bead ruler.

Stringing Products

It's important to choose your stringing product to correspond with the types of beads you are using, as well as the style of project.

Bead design board helps with the placement of beads in a project. By arranging the beads on the work surface, you will quickly know if you have enough materials to create the project, if the balance is pleasing, and if you might encounter any design or assembly challenges.

Crimp beads are tiny thin-walled metal beads, often used to anchor the stringing material to the clasp. They can be found in a variety of diameters. The number of strands used in a project will dictate the diameter of a needed crimp bead. More strands will require a larger crimp bead. Crimp beads can be round or tube-shaped.

In use, the stringing material is fed through the crimp bead, through the clasp and back through the crimp bead. The crimp bead is crushed, and the metal clamps down onto the stringing material, preventing it from coming undone. With heavier projects, sometimes two crimp beads are used to secure the clasp. Often, a designer uses a bead with a slightly larger hole at the end of the project in order to hide the crimp beads after they are crushed.

Gold or silver crimp tubes are used to anchor stringing materials, usually to jump rings or clasps. Using good-quality crimp beads should be a high priority, for when a crimp breaks, your project will literally fall apart. Crimp beads should match the color of your findings in your project for a professional look.

Crimping pliers have two grooves machined into the jaws and are made specifically for crushing and closing crimps.

Metal findings of good quality add to the overall value of any piece of jewelry. These are the parts of the piece of jewelry that are handled the most, as the wearer takes the piece on and off.

Soft Flex™ Wire is composed of several micro-woven, stainless steel wires, this wire is also coated with nylon to increase its durability. It is available in many colors, including 24-karat gold.

Soft Touch™ Wire was developed for its strength and flexibility. The weight and uniformity of the beads you are using is your guide in selecting a diameter of this wire. The heavier the beads, the heavier the wire should be to support the beads. Also as a rule of thumb, the thicker the wire, the less susceptible it is to breakage resulting from abrasion. Use thinner wire for lightweight projects, such as pearls.

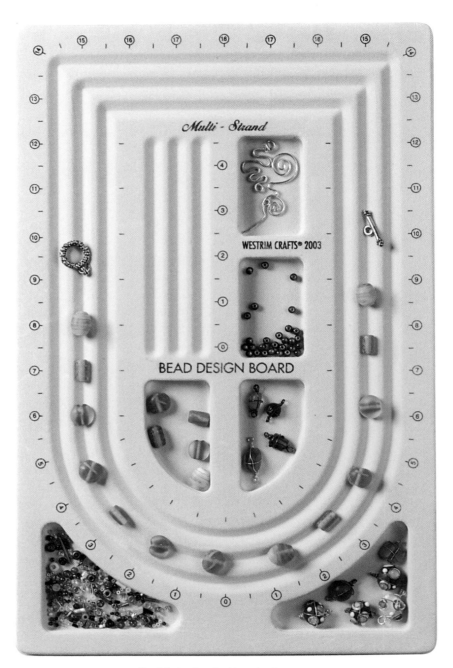

Bead design board with project in progress.

Fishing line and monofilament cords are generally not recommended for use in creating jewelry, as they tend to stretch out and become brittle with time.

A variety of clasps, clockwise from top left: Spring ring; four styles of lobster claw clasps; screw clasp; three styles of round toggle clasps; decorative lock-and-key toggle clasp; magnetic clasp; two-strand slide clasp; friction clasp; and four styles of hook-and-eye clasps.

Clasps

The quality of the clasp used on any jewelry piece is a good indication to the quality of the materials used in the project. Be sure to use the best quality you can, and the perceived value of your piece will increase.

Bead caps and cones can be added to a bead to transform its look completely or draw attention to that particular bead.

An assortment of metal cones and bead caps, clockwise from left: bead cones with spring insert; large and small bead caps; and metal cone set with spring ring clasp.

Decorative lock-and-key clasps are one example of many different styles of toggle clasps. There also are hearts, teapots, stars, flowers, and more. Again, the same principle of weight applies to this style of clasp to keep it closed when worn.

Friction clasps are held together by the friction of the two parts sliding together. The heaviness of the project will be a key consideration before deciding to use this style of clasp, as a heavy project will cause it to slide apart and fall off. Several ounces is the maximum weight for this style of clasp.

Hook-and-eye clasps are easy to make with wire, but also are available in a number of styles. They are easy to use and attractive on a variety of projects. This style of clasp is not best used on bracelets, as it is not very secure, since the hook is always open.

Lobster claw clasps are widely used in jewelry making. They are available in a wide range of sizes and shapes, so it's important to select a size that is in proportion to your project.

Magnetic clasps are extremely easy to operate. The strong magnets embedded inside literally cause the halves of the clasp to jump together as the jewelry piece is put on. These clasps do have a limit as to the amount of weight they can secure, which is only found out through trial-and-error. If your project exceeds that weight, the wearer might be surprised as their jewelry falls off. Combining magnetic clasps and safety chains on lightweight bracelets is a safe design solution, as the magnetic clasp makes it extremely easy to put the bracelet on, and the safety chain slides over the hand and keep the bracelet from falling off if the wearer makes a sudden movement.

Metal cones are particularly effective for ending multiple strands of beads. They add an attractive and secure ending to a project. Depending on the style of metal cone, the end of the project can be secured with a wire inserted through the cone, followed with pulling the ends of the project up inside.

Round toggle clasps are extremely popular and are available in a wide variety of sizes. A caution with toggle clasps: They are best used on projects with some weight, as the weight of the jewelry pulling on each side of the clasp keeps it securely fastened.

Screw clasps have two parts that screw together to close. The operation of this style of clasp stresses the stringing material attached to the clasp, since the clasp must be constantly rotated back and forth for the wearer to put it on and take it off.

Spring ring clasps are usually the most economical, though are often associated with inexpensive jewelry. They can be difficult for someone with stiff fingers to operate.

Clockwise, from top right: adhesive posts with clutches featuring comfort disks; ear posts; half-ball posts with rings; endless hoop rings; kidney wire earrings; half-ball ear clips with rings; ear screws with rings; two styles of lever-back ear wires; and three styles of French ear wires.

Earring Findings

Earrings are easy to assemble and quick to make. Be sure to use quality findings, as many wearers experience great sensitivity to base metal earrings.

Adhesive posts with clutches are well-suited for easily attaching a flat-backed item to them by peeling off the liner to the adhesive pad. The clutches often have comfort disks attached that help to stabilize the ear lobe, particularly if the earring is heavy. Use lightweight materials when depending on the adhesive pad to hold the decorative element in place.

Ear posts require glue to attach a decorative element. Use a glue that is specifically made to attach your decorative element to the metal finding.

Ear screws with rings are designed for the wearer with unpierced ears and are traditional in style.

A variety of earring styles featuring French ear wires.

French ear wires are also known as fish hook style because of their distinctive shape. The style without the ring allows the jewelry designer to slip on a decorative bead before creating the loop for a dangle.

Endless hoop rings are simple and elegant findings that work well with added beads or other dangles.

Eye pins are thin wires with small loops on one end, with the "eye" specifically referring to the loop. Particularly useful in creating earring dangles, eye pins enable you to simply slide on a bead (or a few beads), put a decorative loop or spiral on the other end, and attach the eye to the ring on an earring wire.

Half-ball ear clips with rings give wearers with unpierced ears the look of pierced earrings. The ring is a connection point for attaching a decorative element.

Half-ball posts with rings provide a point of attachment (a ring) for an earring dangle.

Head pins are available with a small, flat cap or decorative element. They are an additional option when attaching dangling elements to your jewelry projects.

Kidney wire earrings are easy to create in wire and offer many design opportunities.

Lever-back ear wires are elegant, yet secure, and comfortable to wear. The wearer flips down the lever on the back of the earring, inserts the wire through the ear, and flips the lever back up to close the earring.

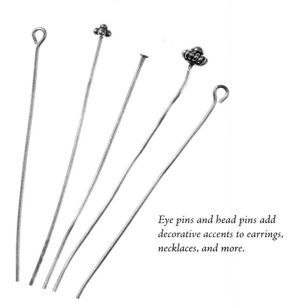

Eye pins and head pins add decorative accents to earrings, necklaces, and more.

Specialty Components

If you would like to create more than necklaces or earrings, using specialty findings will help you achieve this goal.

Earring components are stamped components available in a wide variety of styles that can add value and interest to your earrings.

Eyeglass leash holders are the stretchy rubber ring slips over the end of the eyeglasses when worn.

Jump rings are indispensable components in jewelry-making, as they are used to connect wire segments together or to attach earring findings to dangles or tassels, and so much more.

Split rings are more secure than jump rings, as they allow you to securely connect two components.

From top: two styles of earring components and eyeglass leash holder findings.

CHAPTER 4

WIRE FINDINGS

Wire is an extremely versatile material that can truly personalize any project. You can create findings, earring wires, embellish focal beads, and construct exquisite jewelry entirely out of wire.

Creating Your Own Findings

Being in creative control of your jewelry empowers you to develop and create a signature style. By learning to make your own findings you aren't dependent on what a store, catalog, or Web site might have to offer. Additionally, if you are using colored wires, you will be able to coordinate the finding color to the project.

Wrapped Loop

The wrapped loop is a basic element in wire working and is often an important connector of design elements in a piece of jewelry. The uses include making a dangle or connecting two loops, such as the loop on a charm or a dangle for an earring wire.

> When making a wrapped loop as part of a clasp, be sure to examine the other side of the closure to determine the size of the loop needed for the closure to go through. If the loop is too small, the closure will not work, and you will need to create another.

1. Working off the spool, cut and file the end of the wire.

2. Determine the size of the loop you wish to create and where on the tapered jaws of the round nose pliers you will bend the wire. Grip wire with round nose pliers about 1½" from the end. Use your thumb to bend the wire over the lower jaw of the pliers while rotating the hand holding the pliers in the opposite direction.

> In the beginning when you are making several wrapped loops for a project, it is helpful to use a permanent marker to put a small mark on your round nose plier's jaws at the place where you will want to bend the wire. This will help you to create several loops of the same diameter.

3. Grip the loop with the chain nose pliers and flatten the loop gently.

4. Hold the loop with the chain nose pliers and with your other hand, wrap the wire tightly around the base of the loop. Rotate the hand holding the pliers in the opposite direction. Put two or three wraps of wire at the base of the first loop.

5. Cut off the excess wire tail with the flush cutters and file the end. You can stop here and use this loop as an eye pin for an earring dangle or other jewelry project.

6. To continue and create the loop portion of a clasp, put another wrapped loop on the other end. Grip wire with the tips of the chain nose pliers at the base of the wraps you just added. Put a right-angle bend into the wire.

7. Grip the wire with the round nose pliers just above the right-angle bend and wrap the wire around the pliers' jaw.

8. Flatten the loop with the chain nose pliers and then hold the loop securely, as in step 4. Tightly wind the tail two or three times around wire at base of loop.

9. Clip off the excess tail and file the cut end.

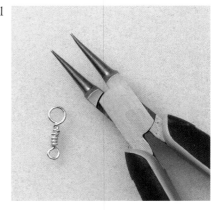

Simple Hook

It's easy to create a basic hook to close a necklace or bracelet, and the same technique can be used for making a basic fish hook-style earring finding.

1. Cut a 5" length of wire and file both cut ends.

2. Grip one end of the wire with the tips of the round nose pliers. Rotate the pliers to put a small loop on the end of the wire.

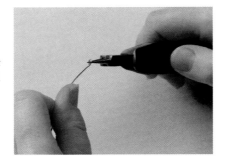

3. Grip the wire with the chain nose pliers, so the wire crosses the jaws near the joint of the pliers, and the edges of the jaws are at the base of the loop. Use your thumb to press the wire against the side of the pliers, creating a right-angle bend in the wire.

4. Grip the wire with the chain nose pliers about ⅜" from the last bend and use your finger to press the wire against the side of the pliers, creating another right-angle bend in the wire.

5. Grip the wire with the chain nose pliers about 1-¼" below the last bend and put a right-angle bend in the wire.

6. Grip the wire just below this bend with the round nose pliers and put a small loop just below the bend.

7. Cut the wire where it intersects to complete the loop and then use the chain nose pliers to flatten the loop.

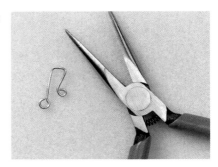

8. Harden the simple hook by hammering it on an anvil.

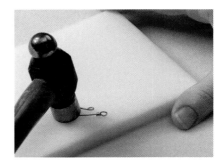

9. To make the loop more secure, you could opt to put a wrapped loop on the end. If you put a wrapped loop on the end, be sure to file the end after cutting off the excess wire.

French Ear Wire Variation

1. After step 4 of the simple hook instructions, cut the wire about 2" below the last bend.

2. File the cut end.

3. Grip the end of the wire with the chain nose pliers and put a slight bend in the wire.

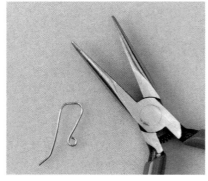

Hook Clasp

Create a durable and strong hook as part of a clasp that has a wrapped loop on one end to securely attach the finding to a piece of jewelry.

1. Cut a 6" length of wire and file the cut ends.

2. Grip the center of wire with the tips of the chain nose pliers and bend wire in half.

3. Grip both wires about 1" below the bend and bend the wire up at a right-angle, just below the pliers. Continue gripping both wires and use your thumb to begin to wrap the bent wire around the other wire, adding two wraps.

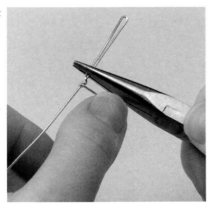

4. Cut the wire and carefully file the end.

5. Grip the end of the first bend with the round nose pliers and rotate the pliers so the bend curves up slightly.

6. Grip the wires with the chain nose pliers about ⅜" beyond the first bend and put a right-angle bend in the wires. Keep gripping the wires with the chain nose pliers and use your thumb to shape the wire.

7. Grip the remaining wire with the round nose pliers just below the wraps of the first wire. Bend the wire around one of the jaws of the pliers so it forms a loop. Grip the loop with chain nose pliers so it lines up with the other wire. Wrap the tail around the wire, just below the first wraps, cut off any excess wire, and file the cut end.

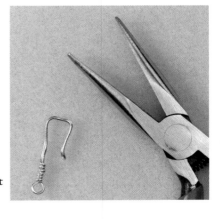

8. Use the chain nose pliers to adjust or straighten the wires, if necessary.

"S" Hook Clasp

This elegant clasp is easy to create with a little practice.

1. Cut a 6" length of wire and file the cut ends.

2. Grip one end of the wire with the tip of the round nose pliers and put a small loop on the end.

3. Move the round nose pliers about ½" away from the loop and grip the wire at the base of the jaws. Bend the wire around the jaws to create a hook.

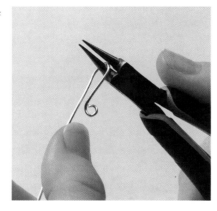

4. Grip the wire at the base of the round nose pliers about ¾" below that bend and bend the wire over the jaws.

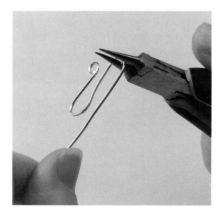

5. About ½" beyond that bend, grip the wire with the tips of the round nose pliers and put a small loop in the wire.

6. Cut off the excess wire where it crosses and then use the chain nose pliers to flatten the loops and adjust the "S" hook.

7. Work-harden the "S" hook clasp by hammering the finding on the anvil with a metal-faced hammer.

Flat Coil/Spiral

A classic design element, spirals are used as a decorative embellishment on earrings, bracelets, or necklaces. Spirals may also be used with a hook to become part of a clasp or to embellish the end of a head pin.

1. Cut a 5" length of wire and file both ends.

2. Working with the wire, firmly grip the end of wire with the tip of the round nose pliers. Rotate the pliers to put a very small loop on the wire end.

3. Grip this loop with round nose pliers and hold the pliers so the wire is horizontal and the tips of the pliers are pointing at the ceiling. Gently bend the wire to curve around the loop.

4. Adjust pliers by moving them down the wire about 1/16" and bend the wire to follow the curve of the loop.

5. Continue moving pliers and bending the wire, as in step 4, until the spiral is the size you desire. With practice, coiling can be done in a smooth, continuous motion.

6. If desired, hammer the spiral to work-harden the wire.

Square or Triangular Coil Variation

1. Working with the wire, use the chain nose pliers in place of the round nose pliers and press wire firmly against the jaws to create an angular bend.

2. Grip the upper edge of wire, just past the bend and continue bending wire around pliers.

3. Repeat step 2 until the square coil is the size desired.

4. If desired, hammer wiggles to flatten, work-harden, and for texture.

Paddle Head Pin

This is an elegant way to create a dangle earring wire.

1. Cut a 3" length of wire and file one end smooth.

2. File the other end so it is rounded.

3. Place the rounded end on an anvil and hammer the tip of the wire. It should begin to flatten and spread out. Continue hammering until the wire is flared. This flare is what will stop your bead from falling off the wire.

4. File the edges of the flattened end smooth.

Two paddle head pins, one with a bead.

Decorative Wire Components

Any shape that can be drawn can be replicated in wire. Once you're familiar with wire work you will be able to begin making a variety of shapes to add visual interest to clasps, necklaces, earrings and more.

Wire components, clockwise from top: leaf, spirals, wiggles, dragonfly, and hand.

Leaf Hook Clasp

The leaf clasp will add a whimsical touch to any project.

1. Working off a spool of 20-gauge wire, cut off the tip of the end and file it smooth.

2. Put a hook clasp on the end of the wire, as instructed on page 37, but do not cut off the excess wire, as noted in step 7. Use your fingers to put a gentle curve into the wire just below the clasp.

3. Determine the length of your leaf (this one is about 2"). Use the tip of the round nose pliers to put a sharp bend into the wire.

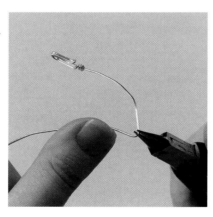

4. Bend the wire around to create the outside leaf shape with your fingers, bringing the end of the wire around to cross over the base of the hook clasp.

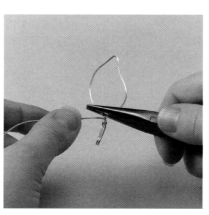

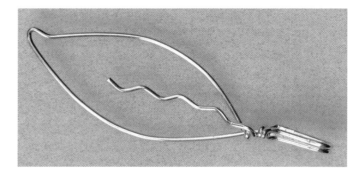

5. With the needle nose pliers, grip the wires where they cross. Wrap the wire around the base of the hook clasp two times to anchor. Bend the tail of the wire so it is pointing toward the tip of the leaf and then add a small right-angle bend in the wire.

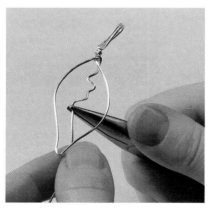

6. Cut off the excess wire and file the end smooth.

Spiral

Spirals are a common motif in jewelry and art. Adding wire spirals as dangles, charms, or connectors to many projects adds an elegant touch.

1. Cut a 6" length of wire and file both ends.

2. Use the tips of the round nose pliers to begin bending a curve into the wire, working with the wire.

3. Continue gently bending the wire against the outside edge of the round nose pliers, and moving the pliers down the wire. Stop periodically to adjust the forming coil, making sure that the spiral is symmetrical.

4. When you have about ½" of wire left, determine if you want to anchor the end. To anchor the end, use the needle nose pliers

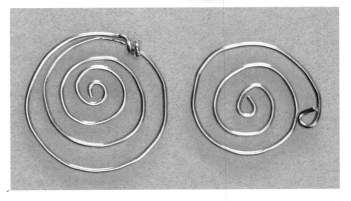

to put a right-angle bend into the wire. Grip the wire with the round nose pliers just above the bend and bend the end of the wire around the coil.

5. Cut off any excess wire and file.

Wiggle

Add additional texture and decorative elements to your jewelry. Wiggles can be created freehand or by using a jig. It's best to create wiggles by working off the spool of 18- or 20-gauge wire.

1. Working off the spool, grip the end of wire with the tip of the round nose pliers and rotate the pliers to bend the wire around the jaws to form a loop.

2. Continue using the round nose pliers to add random bends to the wire.

3. If desired, hammer wiggles with a jewelry hammer and anvil to flatten.

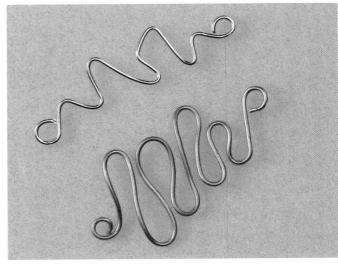

Wiggles with bends created with needle nose pliers (top) and with round nose pliers. Round nose pliers result in curving, rounded wiggles. Needle nose pliers result in angular wiggles.

Dragonfly Clasp

The dragonfly clasp is a trendy component. Use this project as a model to create other similar shapes, such as a butterfly.

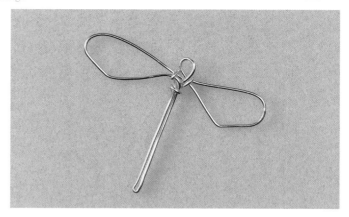

1. Cut a 10" length of 20-gauge wire and file cut ends.

2. Measure 4" from one end and grip it there with the tip of the round nose pliers. Bend the wire over the tip of the pliers to create the tail of the dragonfly.

3. About 1¼" up from the bend, put a right-angle bend into one of the wires, bending it away from the other wire.

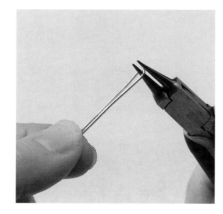

4. About 1" from that bend, gently grip the wire with the base of the round nose pliers and begin bending the wire around the pliers. Move the pliers down the wire slightly to increase the diameter of the curve. Continue bending the wire until the end crosses the other wire right at the bend. This is the first wing.

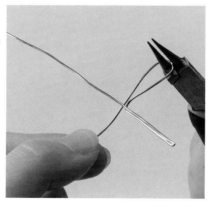

5. About 1" from that bend, gently grip the wire with the base of the round nose pliers and begin bending the wire around the pliers. Move the pliers down the wire slightly to increase the diameter of the curve. Continue bending the wire until the end crosses the other wire right at the bend. This is the second wing.

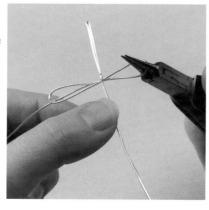

6. With the round nose pliers, grip the intersection where the wings connect with the tail. Use the wire that created the wings and bend it up above the wings and around the tips of the pliers to form the small loop that will be the head. Bend that wire down along side of the dragonfly tail.

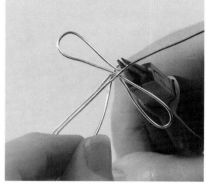

7. Firmly hold the dragonfly with your fingers and wrap the loose end of the wire around the body to anchor the head and wings.

8. Neaten up the bends with the needle nose pliers.

9. Use the wire cutters to cut off any excess wire, as shown, and then file the ends.

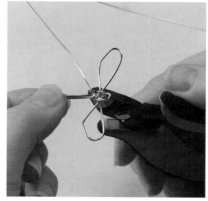

Wire Hand

I particularly enjoy making the hand wire component. It is used in many of the projects in this book.

1. Working off the spool of 20-gauge wire, cut off the tip and file the end.

2. Grip the wire about 3" from the end with the tip of the needle nose pliers. Use your fingers to bend the wire around the pliers jaws, forming a "U" shape. With the tip of the pliers, grip the wire on the side of the "U" that is still attached to the spool about ⅜" from the bottom of the "U". Bend the wire around the pliers, forming a "V" shape. This is the "thumb" of the wire hand.

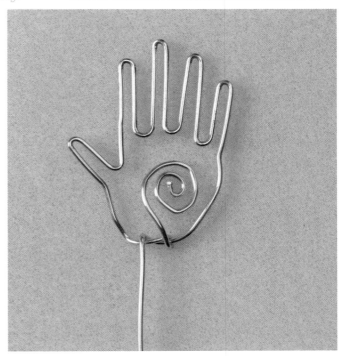

3. With the tip of the pliers, grip the wire on the wide of the "V" that is still attached to the spool about 1" from the bottom of the "V". Bend the wire around the pliers, forming a "U" shape. Grip the wire on the other side of the "U" shape about ½" from the bottom of the "U". Bend another "U" into the wire. This is the "index finger" of the wire hand.

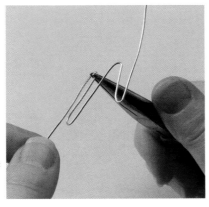

4. Continue gripping and bending "U" shapes into the wire until you have the desired shape of the human hand. Be sure the "middle finger" is slightly longer than the "index finger" and the "ring finger" is slightly shorter that the middle, and so on.

5. Grip the wire at the base of the "pinky finger" and just put a slight outward bend into the wire.

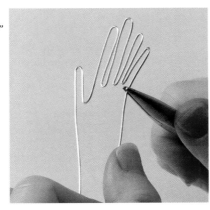

6. Bend the wire around to form the "palm" of the hand. Bend the wire around the other wire to anchor.

7. Cut off the spool, leaving about a 2" tail, and then file the cut end.

8. Grip the end with the round nose pliers and add a spiral. Refer back to the instructions for making a spiral on page 41, if necessary.

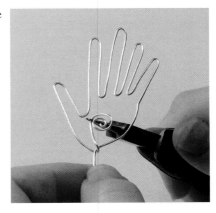

9. Use the needle nose pliers to neaten up the bends in the fingers and adjust the fingers.

10. Optional: You may want to work-harden this wire element so it does not bend out of shape.

From Jump Rings to Beads

The Twist 'n Curl tool can be used to create simple jump rings or flower-like wire beads. You will always work off the wire spool when creating coils and beads with the tool.

To create a coil for jump rings:

1. Insert the end of the wire through the hole in the Twist 'n Curl handle.

2. While holding the tool horizontally, spin the handle to create tight coils of wire. These coils should line up right next to each other on the mandrel.

To create a Second Step Twist 'n Curl bead:

1. Create a coil that is nearly the length of the mandrel.

2. Remove the coil from the mandrel and file cut end.

3. Cut off the excess wire from the other end and file cut end.

4. Thread the end of the wire through the coil and through the hole in the handle.

5. Begin to spin the handle again, putting three or four wraps onto the mandrel.

6. Tightly hold the wire at the base of the coil and begin winding the coil around the mandrel until the coil is completely wrapped, adding three to four more wraps at the base of the bead.

7. Push the wire up to the top of the mandrel and cut off the excess wire.

8. Cut off the wire at the top and slide bead off mandrel.

To create a Third Step Twist 'n Curl bead:

(Be sure to create a very long wire coil when making this bead.)

1. Thread the wire through the center of the Second Step Twist 'n Curl bead.

2. Anchor the end in the handle and add three to four wraps to the mandrel.

3. Slide the bead up to the wraps and begin winding the bead around the mandrel, adding three or four more wire wraps at the end to anchor. Note: You will have to hold the wire very tightly to force the Second Step Twist 'n Curl bead to wrap around the mandrel.

4. Push the wire up to the top of the mandrel and cut off the excess wire.

5. Cut off the wire at the top and slide bead off mandrel.

Twist 'n Curl Bracelet

This bracelet and the two projects that follow it were created using the same materials: silver, wire, and beads. The Twist 'n Curl is such a simple tool, yet the beads you can make with wire look quite complicated. This project can be dressed up or down, depending on the types of beads used.

Materials

36" 20-gauge sterling silver
   dead-soft wire

20" 18-gauge sterling silver
   half-hard wire

7 6mm to 8mm lampwork beads*

Twist 'n Curl tool
   with small round mandrel

Wire cutters

Round nose pliers

Needle nose pliers

Flat file

Ruler

*The beads for this project were
   created by Kim Ballor.

Finished size: 7½"

Instructions

1. With 20-gauge wire, create six Second Step Twist 'n Curl (TNC) pieces, as instructed on page 44.

2. Working off the spool of 18-gauge wire, cut the tip and file the end.

3. Put a hook clasp on the end of the 18-gauge wire, as instructed on page 37.

4. Measure 12" from the base of the hook clasp, cut the wire at this point, and file the end.

5. Slide a lampwork bead onto the 12" length, followed by a TNC bead, and another lampwork bead.

6. Grip the wire on either side of the lampwork beads and slide them toward the TNC bead to compress the TNC beads so the wrapped tails are pushed inside the bead, as shown.

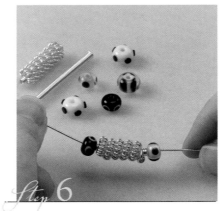

7. Repeat steps 5 and 6 until all beads are on the wire.

8. Slide the beads up to the hook clasp and put a wrapped loop on the other end, as instructed on page 37. Be sure the diameter of the loop will accept the hook.

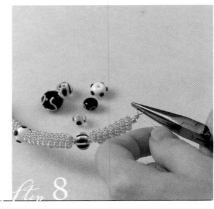

Flat Coil Bracelet

Building on how to use small focal beads in a variety of ways, the flat coils create visual interest, while the beads create the dimension.

Materials

50" 18-gauge sterling silver half-hard wire

9 6mm to 8mm lampwork beads*

Wire cutters

Round nose pliers

Needle nose pliers

Flat file

Ruler

*The beads for this project were created by Kim Ballor.

Finished size: 7½"

Instructions

1. Cut a 10" length of wire and file the ends.

2. Find the center of the wire and grip it with the round nose pliers about ⅛" from the end of the jaws. Bend one end of the wire around one of the jaws and then bend the other end in the opposite direction, as shown below.

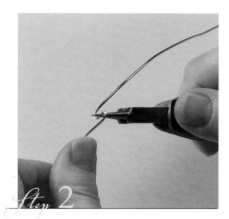

3. Continue bending the wire ends in opposite directions until a flat coil is formed.

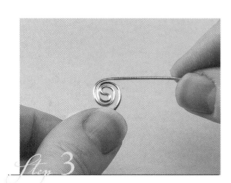

4. Use the needle nose pliers to bend one wire at a right-angle to the flat coil. Repeat for the other side.

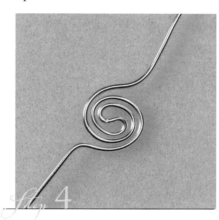

5. Add a lampwork bead to one end and secure the bead with a wrapped loop, as instructed on page 35. Repeat for the other end.

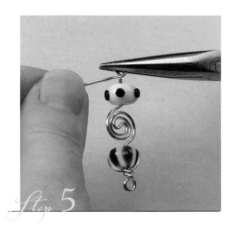

6. Make another flat coil and add a lampwork bead to one end.

7. Begin to add a wrapped loop, but just after you add the loop part, slip the wire through the loop of the first segment and then wrap the base of the loop.

8. Cut off the excess wire and file the end.

9. Repeat steps 1 through 8 until you have four flat coil segments.

10. Cut a 5" length of wire and put a wrapped loop on one end, attaching the loop to the end of the connected flat coil segments.

11. Slide on a lampwork bead and put a wrapped loop (with a large loop) on the other end.

12. Make a simple hook, as instructed on page 36, and attach it to the other end of the bracelet.

In step 9, create more flat coil segments if additional length is desired.

Bicone Spiral Bracelet

This bracelet has great visual impact, yet it is still lightweight to wear. Increasing the wire gauge will result in a completely new look. Be sure to practice making the spiral on inexpensive wire first.

Materials

36" 18-gauge sterling silver
  half-hard wire

9 6mm to 8mm lampwork beads*

Wire cutters

Round nose pliers

Needle nose pliers

Flat file

Ruler

Permanent marker

*The beads for this project were
  created by Kim Ballor.

Finished size: 7½"

Instructions

1. Cut a 7" length of wire and file the ends.

2. Find the center of the wire and use the marker to mark this spot.

3. Use the tip of the round nose pliers to grip the end of the wire and put a tight spiral on the wire, as instructed on page 41, continuing until you reach the mark.

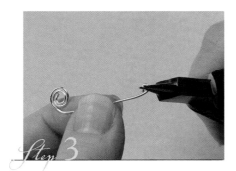

4. Put a matching spiral on the other end of the wire and use the needle nose pliers to flatten both spirals.

5. Use the needle nose pliers to bend the coils over, as though your were closing a book.

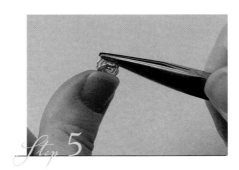

6. Grip the innermost wire spiral on one side with the tip of the needle nose pliers and begin to pull the wire out, as shown.

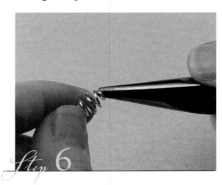

7. Repeat step 6 for the other side of the bead.

8. Use the needle nose pliers to adjust the wire until the coils are evenly spaced apart.

9. Repeat steps 1 through 8 seven more times until you have eight bicone spiral beads.

Bracelet Assembly Instructions

1. Cut a 10" length of wire and file cut ends.

2. Put a simple hook on one end, as instructed on page 36.

3. Slide on a lampwork bead, followed by a bicone spiral bead, continuing in this pattern until all the beads are added.

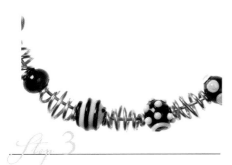

4. Slide the beads down the wire toward the hook and add a loop to finish, as instructed on page 35. Make sure that the diameter of the loop will accept the hook.

5. Cut of any excess wire and file the end.

Bright Blue TNC Necklace

This necklace uses the same TNC bead-making techniques used in the Twist 'n Curl Bracelet, page 45. It is made unique by the intense blue in Donna Kato's polymer clay bead, which is accented by Paula Radke's dichroic beads and the coated copper wire.

Materials

24-gauge turquoise-coated copper Artistic Wire

24-gauge non-tarnish brass-coated copper Artistic Wire

18-gauge blue-coated copper Artistic Wire

10 blue dichroic 4mm glass beads*

Oval polymer clay focal bead*

Twist 'n Curl tool with small round mandrel

Wire cutters

Round nose pliers

Needle nose pliers

Flat file

*The dichroic beads were created by Paula Radke and the polymer clay focal bead by Donna Kato.

Finished size: 22"

Instructions

1. Create eight Second Step Twist 'n Curl (TNC) beads, as instructed on page 44, by coiling the turquoise and non-tarnish brass wires together at the same time when making the first coil. Modify the shape of the beads by gently gripping the bead on either side of the center of the bead and slowly rotating your hands in opposite directions.

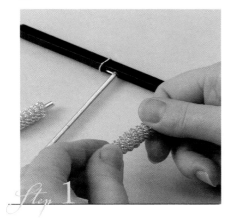

2. Move your hands to the end and continue to gently rotate the bead ends in opposite directions. Reshape the coils as necessary to maintain the overall shape. Modify all eight TNC beads.

3. Cut a 3" length of 18-gauge blue wire and file both ends.

4. Grip the end of the wire at the base of the round nose pliers and put a loop on one end.

5. Slide a dichroic bead onto the wire, grip the wire with the base of the round nose pliers about ⅛" away from bead, and use your fingers to put a loop on the other end.

6. Cut off the excess wire.

7. Adjust the loops with needle nose pliers to be snug against the bead.

8. Repeat steps 3 through 7 with the other nine dichroic beads and all eight TNC beads.

9. Using the 18-gauge blue wire, make a large spiral, as instructed on page 41, with a wrapped loop on the end, as detailed on page 35.

10. Make a hook clasp out of the same wire, referring to the instructions on page 37, if necessary.

11. Cut 12" of blue 18-gauge wire and file both ends.

12. Put an anchored spiral on one end, slide the focal bead onto the wire, and put a wrapped loop on the other end.

13. Open the loop of one of the dichroic bead segments and hook it through the spiral of the focal bead. Attach a TNC bead to the other side. Continue this pattern, adding four more TNC bead segments and finishing with one more dichroic bead segment and the hook clasp.

14. Attach a dichroic bead segment to the other side of the focal bead, and then a TNC bead. Continue adding beads in this pattern until you have added all of the bead segments. Attach the spiral side of the clasp at the end.

Wire "Interview" Necklace

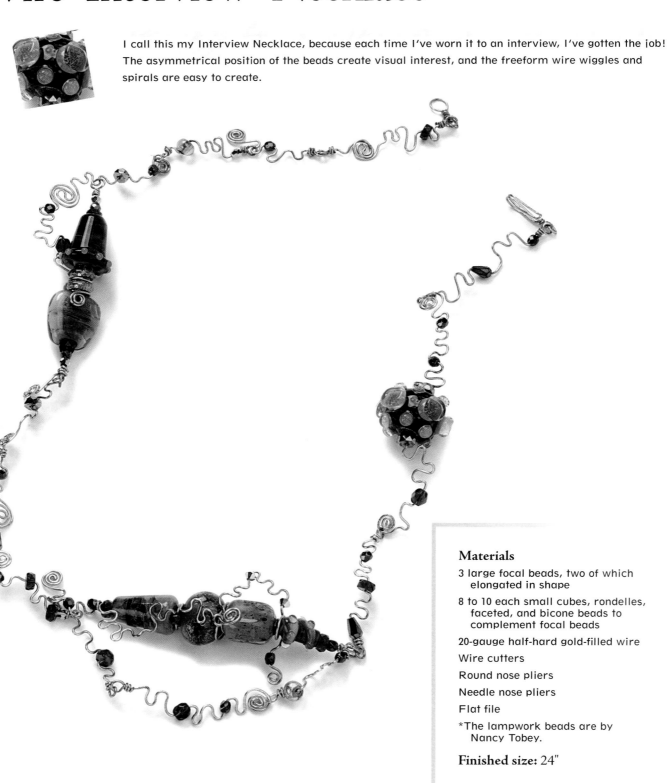

I call this my Interview Necklace, because each time I've worn it to an interview, I've gotten the job! The asymmetrical position of the beads create visual interest, and the freeform wire wiggles and spirals are easy to create.

Materials

3 large focal beads, two of which elongated in shape

8 to 10 each small cubes, rondelles, faceted, and bicone beads to complement focal beads

20-gauge half-hard gold-filled wire

Wire cutters

Round nose pliers

Needle nose pliers

Flat file

*The lampwork beads are by Nancy Tobey.

Finished size: 24"

Instructions

1. Cut an 8" length of wire and file both ends.

2. Put a hook clasp on one end and slide two small seed beads onto the wire.

3. Put a small wrapped loop on the other end of the wire, as instructed on page 35.

4. Use the round nose pliers to add several curves and bends to the wire, making sure to position the seed beads away from each other as you work from one end toward the other end.

5. Cut another 8" length of wire and file both ends.

6. Put a large wrapped loop on one end and slide several small seed beads onto the wire.

7. Repeat steps 3 and 4 for this piece of wire.

To embellish the elongated focal beads:

1. Cut a 12" length of wire and file both ends.

2. Put a small spiral on one end, as instructed on page 41, and slide on five or six small seed beads.

3. Slide a seed bead up next to the spiral and using the round nose pliers, begin to bend the wire.

4. Wrap the wire around the bead and add more loops and bends to the wire, sliding up seed beads as you bend the wire, as shown below.

Step 4

5. Wrap and bend the wire until you reach the other end of the bead. Do not attach the end of the wire at this point, just put a spiral onto the end.

6. Working off the spool, cut off the tip of the wire and file the end.

7. Slide a small rondelle, the focal bead, and another rondelle onto the wire and put a small wrapped loop on the end.

8. Cut the wire 3" away from the end of the bead and put another wrapped loop on the other end.

9. Wrap the wire that is embellishing the focal bead around the base of the wrapped loop to anchor.

10. Cut an 8" length of wire and file both ends.

11. Begin to put a small wrapped loop on one end, and before you close the loop, insert the wire through the wrapped loop on the focal bead.

Tip:

When creating wire segments using the freeform bending technique, be sure to double the amount of wire for the desired length of the segment. For example, for a 2" segment, cut a 4" length of wire.

12. Add two seed beads and use the round nose pliers to bend and shape the wire, leaving the last 1" unbent.

13. Bring the end of the wire up to the wire wrapped around the focal bead and attach the end with a loop. This wire should hang below the focal bead.

14. Repeat steps 1 through 9 in this section for the other elongated focal bead, adding several seed beads to embellish.

Step 14

To embellish the third focal bead:

1. For the third focal bead, cut an 8" length of wire and file both ends.

2. Put a wrapped loop on one end and slide on two seed beads, the third focal bead, and two or three more seed beads.

3. Put a wrapped loop on the other end.

4. Use the round nose pliers to bend and shape the wire as desired, making sure to place the focal bead in the center.

To assemble the segments:

1. Arrange the completed segments on your work surface. Determine how many inches and segments are needed to make your necklace the desired length.

2. Add bended wire and seed bead wiggle segments, as instructed on page 41, to achieve the length. Experiment! Try adding the elements you learned in this chapter: flat coils, spirals, or wiggles.

The more "hinges" (areas where the wire segments connect) you can design into a piece of jewelry, the better it will lie when worn.

Gallery

Beaded Wire Bangles

Designed by Louise Duhamel, these bangle bracelets, each measuring 7½" long, incorporate handmade sterling silver beads and wire coils with the beauty of colorful handcrafted lampwork glass. "Each bracelet is unique in character and design," Louise says. "No two are ever alike."

Santa Fe Inspiration

Connie Fox's 7½" bangle was created shortly after her first trip to Santa Fe. The bold use of primary colors in Jamie Dierks' lampwork beads and the Native American stamped silver, coupled with sterling silver wire, are the perfect expression of high desert art so characteristic of this wonderful city.

Aqua Bubble Necklace and Earrings

I created this piece using sterling silver wire, aqua bubbles lampwork beads by Barbara Becker Simon, freshwater pearls, Bali silver beads, and rondelles. These wonderful glass beads look substantial, but they're very light because they're hollow. I love the water-like quality and felt that pearls would be a great accent.

Precious Metal Clay Medallions and Frosted Spirals Necklace

The graphic elements on the PMC medallions I created emphasize the spirals in the gray, frosted lampwork glass beads by Kennebunkport Bead Art to tie these very different materials together. The finished necklace is 20" long.

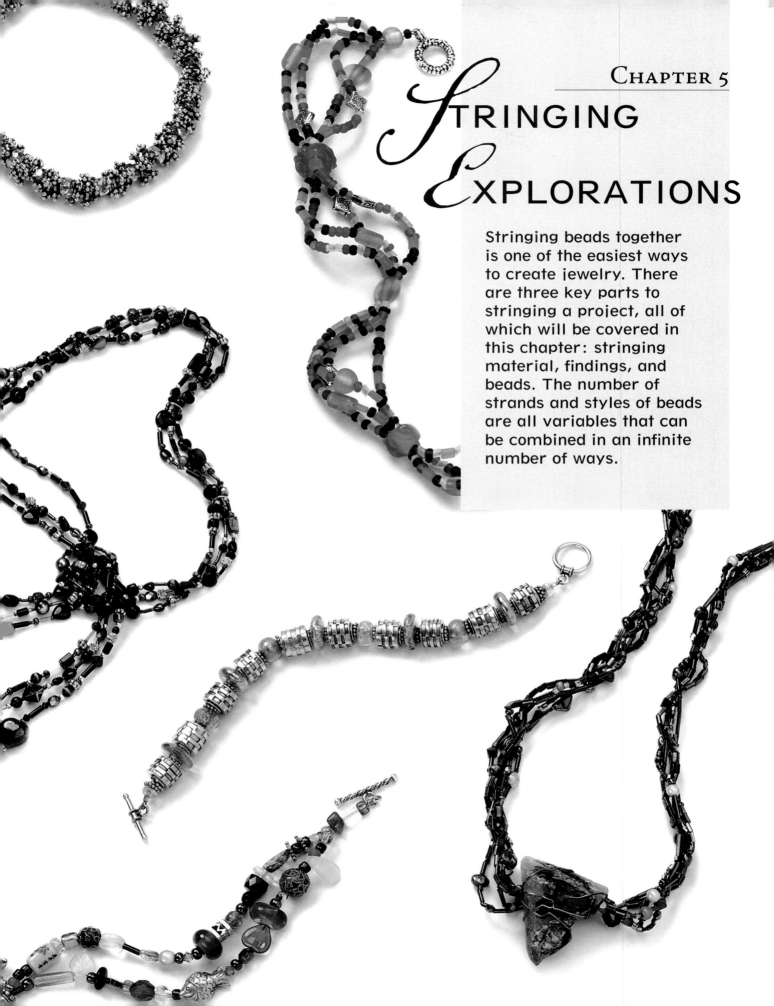

CHAPTER 5

STRINGING EXPLORATIONS

Stringing beads together is one of the easiest ways to create jewelry. There are three key parts to stringing a project, all of which will be covered in this chapter: stringing material, findings, and beads. The number of strands and styles of beads are all variables that can be combined in an infinite number of ways.

Common Jewelry Lengths

Three styles of single-strand necklaces.

The following length suggestions are to be used as a general guide.

Necklaces

Choker: 15" to 16" (depending on the wearer's neck size)
Princess: 18"
Matinee: 20" to 24"
Opera: 28" to 30"
Lariat: 45" or longer

Multi-strand necklaces also follow the sizing above, but involve the additional considerations of uniformity and graduation.

- Uniform length: The strands are all the same length. This design provides the wearer with a couple options. She can twist the strands before closing the clasp for one look, or leave it untwisted.

- Graduated: This look is typically used when creating necklaces that have several strands. Each strand is progressively longer than the one above it. This look is best achieved in projects that have a minimum of three strands. There is no limit to the number of strands that can be used, though a larger number will require a clasp that is suitable to attach each strand and support the weight of the piece.

Bracelets and Cuffs

The size of the wearer's wrist, as well as the size of the beads used in the project can affect the length of a bracelet. A bracelet with large beads, for example, may need to be up to 9" long to fit someone who will wear a traditional 7½" bracelet. Generally, the following guide provides a good starting point.

Small: 6"
Medium: 6½" to 7"
Large: 7½" or longer, depending on the wearer's wrist size.

Arranging the Beads

Composition is the arrangement of the beads on a project. As discussed in Chapter 2, balance, symmetry, color, and size of the beads all contribute to the final appearance of the project.

Pendants direct the eye to the center front of the necklace and can be combined with single-strand necklaces or multiple-strand necklaces. Often, the colors in the pendant are used as a basis for selecting the colors for the beads in the strung portion of the project.

A coordinated string of glass beads complement this antique silver bead with the inclusion of gray-toned glass beads.

Seed pearls, accented with Iolite disks and Swarovski bicone beads, create an elegant necklace with a repetitive pattern.

Natural materials, like those used in the necklace shown here, often require a heavier stringing material for strength and security.

Choosing a Stringing Material

Choose your stringing material after selecting the beads you'll use in the project. The thickness and strength of the stringing material should be matched to the beads. The weight of the beads is one factor in selecting a stringing material. For example, seed beads or pearls do not require a heavy stringing material because they are so lightweight.

In contrast, heavier beads require a much heavier stringing material. The weight of the beads and materials used in a project are an additional consideration in finishing the project, so the strand will not pull free from the clasp or crimp bead. Beads with irregular holes also require a heavier stringing material, as the roughness of the edges of the holes will abrade the stringing material and could cause it to fray and eventually break over time.

There are several brands of nylon-coated stainless steel stringing cords available today. These stringing cords are measured in diameters, as well as the number of micro-fine stainless steel strands that are twisted together in the core. Typically, the smaller the number of strands, the thinner the material, and the more suitable to lighter projects.

It is worth investing in a high-quality stringing material that will withstand the wearing, as well as the weight of the beads.

Nylon or polymer threads are available in a variety of types that are marketed under varying brand names. These materials

have more strength than silk and are available in varying thicknesses and colors.

Silk is often used in stringing pearls. Quality pearls are best strung with a knot between each pearl, as this will prevent all of the pearls from falling off if the strand breaks.

Waxed linen is a traditional jewelry-making material. This stringing material works well with beads that have larger holes, as the waxed linen is much thicker in diameter than silk. The waxed coating assists in keeping the beads from abrading the string.

Avoid using fishing line and related plastic cords, as the plastic is prone to stretching and becoming brittle with age. The last thing you will want is for your project to break or stretch after you've spent time wearing it, have given it as a gift, or sold it.

Getting Started with Stringing

Crimping pliers with finished crimp bead.

As mentioned in Chapter 3, the basic tools you need for stringing include: crimp beads, crimping pliers, stringing cord, clasp, ruler, and beads.

As you arrange your beads, be sure to try several combinations or variations before stringing the beads together; this exercise will help you determine what you like best. Most often it is not the first attempt that I choose to use when stringing beads.

Attaching Clasps with Crimp Beads

To use the crimping pliers:

1. Slide a crimp bead onto the end of the stringing material and then through one part of the clasp.

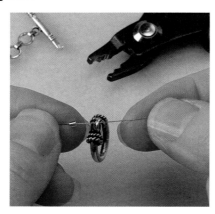

3. Secure the crimp bead by first gripping it with the second groove in the crimping pliers (closest to the joint). Firmly squeeze the pliers closed. If positioned correctly, the crimp should be shaped like a kidney bean—round on one side and indented on the other.

In step 3, it's not necessary to squeeze as hard as you can, as this may damage the crimp and cause it to crumble. Squeezing the tool as if you were giving someone a firm handshake adequately does the job.

2. Thread the cord back through the crimp bead and the last bead you added. Pull on the end of the cord so the crimp bead is nestled between the last bead on the cord and the bead just before the clasp. There should be a little bit of slack so the clasp can flex when opened and closed, but there shouldn't be so much slack that the stringing cord is very noticeable.

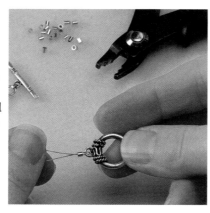

4. Move the crimp to the first groove in the crimping pliers (closest to the tips). Firmly squeeze the pliers closed. If positioned correctly, the crimp should be rounded over, trapping the stringing cord so it cannot pull free.

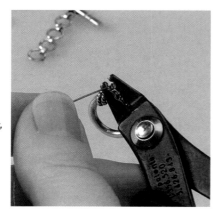

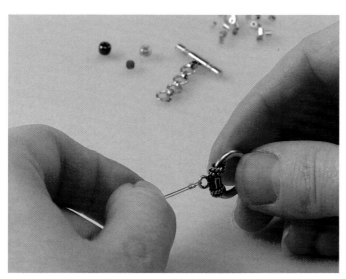

When creating long strands of strung beads, you may want to add a crimp here and there as a safety precaution. If you've added the crimps and the necklace breaks, the beads will not all fall off of the cord.

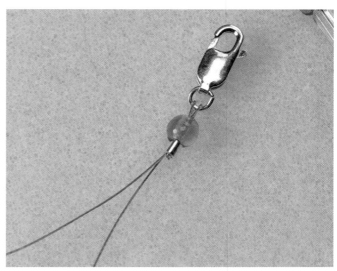

Adding the small round bead just before the clasp incorporates another flex point to your project, which will reduce the wear and stress on the crimp and increase the comfort for the wearer. Also, this will make the piece of jewelry easier to put on and take off.

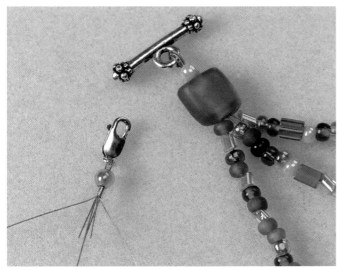

When using more than one strand in a project, treat both strands as one strand and thread them through the crimp bead and clasp at the same time. This step will eliminate the bulk of more than one crimp hanging off the clasp at one time.

If you are stringing extremely heavy beads, you may want to add a second crimp for security. Typically, this second crimp can be hidden if you strategically add a larger-holed bead just before adding the crimps. When the crimp bead is crushed, the hole of the bead rides up over the crimp, effectively hiding it.

A Suite of Spacer Bead Bracelets

Even though these bracelets look very different, it is the beads used that make the difference. The construction is basically the same. I really like wearing these bracelets, as the spacer beads feel great on your arm and are a classy look to accompany any beads.

Materials

115 4mm or 6mm star-shaped Bali silver spacers

5 6mm to 8mm lampwork glass rings

7 small clear glass "E" seed beads

2 silver 2mm crimp beads

Silver toggle clasp

Medium-weight metal-core stringing cord

Bead design board

Wire cutters

Crimping pliers

Finished size: 7½"

Spacer Bead Bracelet with Lampwork Beads

Instructions

1. Cut a 12" length of stringing cord.

2. Use the crimp bead to attach one side of the clasp, as instructed on page 60. Add one small seed bead.

3. Add 15 star spacer beads (filling about 1") and then one glass ring. Add a small clear glass seed bead, which will slip inside the ring so the ring will not slide around on the stringing cord.

4. Add 15 spacer beads and a glass ring with small glass bead until all the spacer beads are used. Add the glass seed bead.

5. Add the crimp bead and the other side of the clasp, as shown, and finish the crimp.

Spacer Bracelet Variations

Option 1: Use five Swarovski clear crystal rondelles in place of the lampwork beads for an elegant evening look.

Option 2: Combine larger barrel-shaped silver beads with dichroic rondelles.

Option 3: Replace the Bali spacer beads with bluestone rondelles for another look.

Option 4: This "ruffled" bracelet without a clasp is a little trickier to assemble, but the effect is gorgeous. Three triangular Bali silver spacer beads are alternated with gray rondelle beads. Instead of using a clasp, the two crimps are strung on the stringing cord and both ends of the stringing cord are threaded through the crimps.

Make sure the bracelet is large enough to roll on over your hand before crushing the crimp. Try to position the crimps under the three spacer beads, as the holes are larger and will hide the crimp bead. Carefully slide the crimping pliers between two spacers to crimp the first crimp. You may want to have someone else hold the other end of the stringing cord to maintain the tension. Once the first crimp is crushed, crush the second crimp in the same manner.

Option 5: Use lampworked beads in place of the Bali spacers.

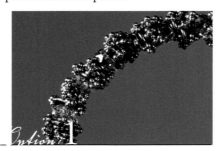

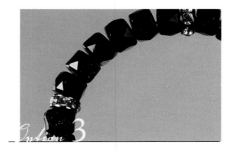

Traveler's Bracelets

These bracelets are fun to make and wear. The name comes from the fact that each bracelet is designed to contain beads from at least five countries, which in this case are China, Bali, USA, India, Czechoslovakia, Thailand, and Peru.

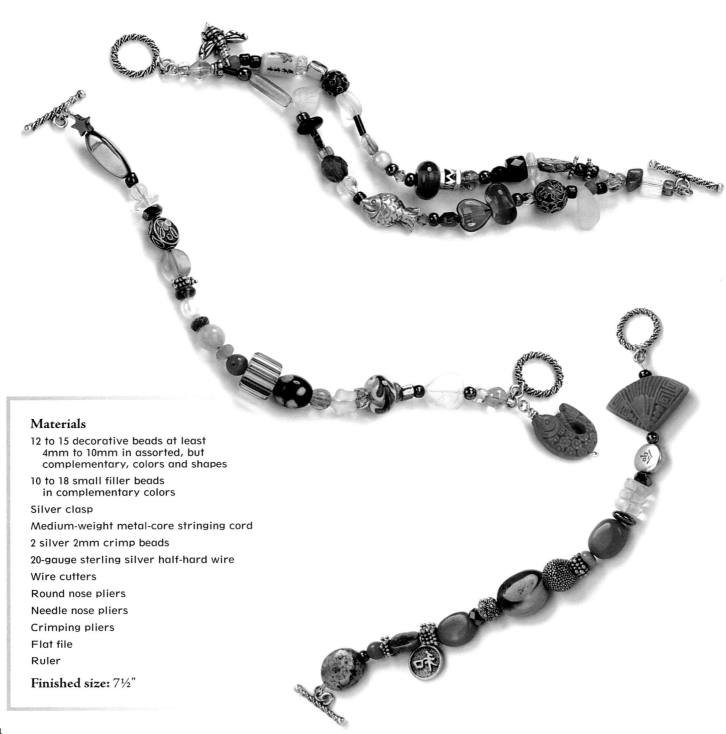

Materials

12 to 15 decorative beads at least 4mm to 10mm in assorted, but complementary, colors and shapes

10 to 18 small filler beads in complementary colors

Silver clasp

Medium-weight metal-core stringing cord

2 silver 2mm crimp beads

20-gauge sterling silver half-hard wire

Wire cutters

Round nose pliers

Needle nose pliers

Crimping pliers

Flat file

Ruler

Finished size: 7½"

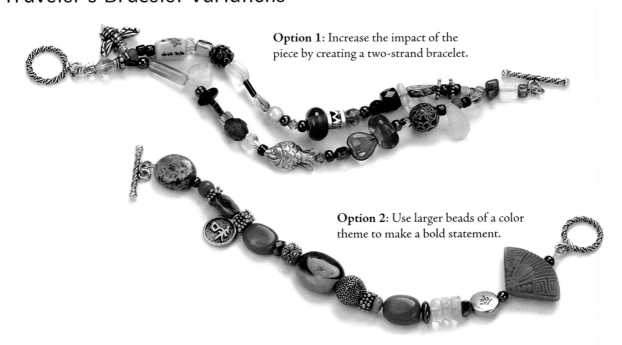

Instructions

To make a dangle:

1. Select a decorative bead to be featured as a dangle and slide it onto the wire.

2. Working off the spool, cut off the end of the wire and file the end.

3. Put a wrapped loop, as detailed on page 35, on the end of the wire.

4. Slide the bead up to the base of the wrapped loop and cut the wire about ⅜" below the bead.

5. File the end of the wire.

6. Grip the wire with the tip of the needle nose pliers and rotate the pliers to bend the wire up toward the bead.

7. Use the needle nose pliers to squeeze the wire up so the end of the wire is pointing into the hole of the decorative bead. This bend of the wire will keep the bead from sliding off the wire.

8. Arrange the remaining beads as desired, paying attention to color, shape, and placement. Try to avoid placing two large beads next to each other, and if your beads have distinct shapes, like a leaf or fish, try to maintain some space between them.

To assemble:

1. Cut a 12" length of stringing cord and attach it to the clasp, using one crimp bead.

2. Slide on all of the beads and then the wire dangle.

3. Attach the other part of the clasp to the other end, using a crimp bead, and slipping the tail of the cord through the last couple of beads.

4. Crush the crimp and cut off any excess wire.

Be sure to place a largish bead near the clasp to give it weight as well as attractiveness. If you place all of the decorative beads near the center of the bracelet, the concentrated weight there will cause the bracelet to slide around on the wearer's wrist so the clasp is on top. By adding a larger bead near the clasp, a metal charm, or attaching a dangle, these elements act as a counterbalance to the weight of the beads on the top of the bracelet.

Traveler's Bracelet Variations

Option 1: Increase the impact of the piece by creating a two-strand bracelet.

Option 2: Use larger beads of a color theme to make a bold statement.

Simply Strung Necklace

This necklace is created using the similar techniques as the Traveler's Bracelets. The combination of a great lampwork bead set and coordinating Swarovski crystals makes this necklace a stunning piece. The amazing thing is how easy it is to assemble. By combining unique beads and the principles of proportion, you will make great jewelry.

Materials

25mm focal lampwork glass bead

6 15mm coordinating secondary
  lampwork glass beads

30 to 40 assorted small beads in colors to
  coordinate with focal beads

Lightweight metal-core stringing cord

18-gauge sterling silver wire "S" clasp

2 sterling silver 18-gauge jump rings

2 silver 2mm crimp beads

Wire cutters

Round nose pliers

Needle nose pliers

Crimping pliers

Flat file

Beading tray

Finished size: 20"

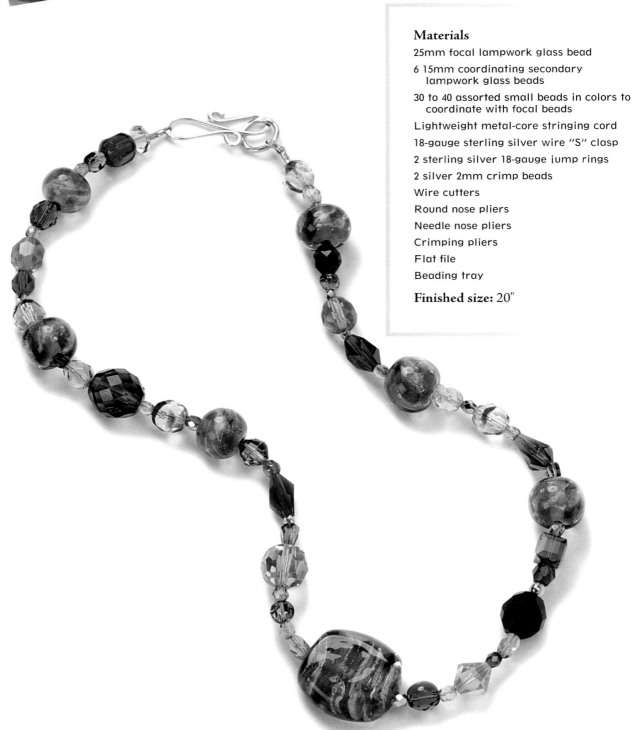

Instructions

1. Create a wire "S" hook clasp, as instructed on page 38.

2. Arrange the beads in the bead tray with the largest lampwork bead in the center. Add the coordinating lampwork beads, three per side at equally spaced increments. Fill in with the smaller coordinating beads.

3. Cut a 24" length of stringing cord.

4. Slide on a crimp bead, loop the cord through one side of the clasp and back through the crimp bead. Crush the crimp bead with the crimping pliers.

5. Add the beads in the arranged order from the bead tray.

6. Once all the beads are added, thread the cord through a crimp bead, through the jump ring and back through the crimp bead and the last couple of beads that were added. Crush the crimp bead with the crimping pliers.

7. Cut off the excess wire.

Simply Strung Variations

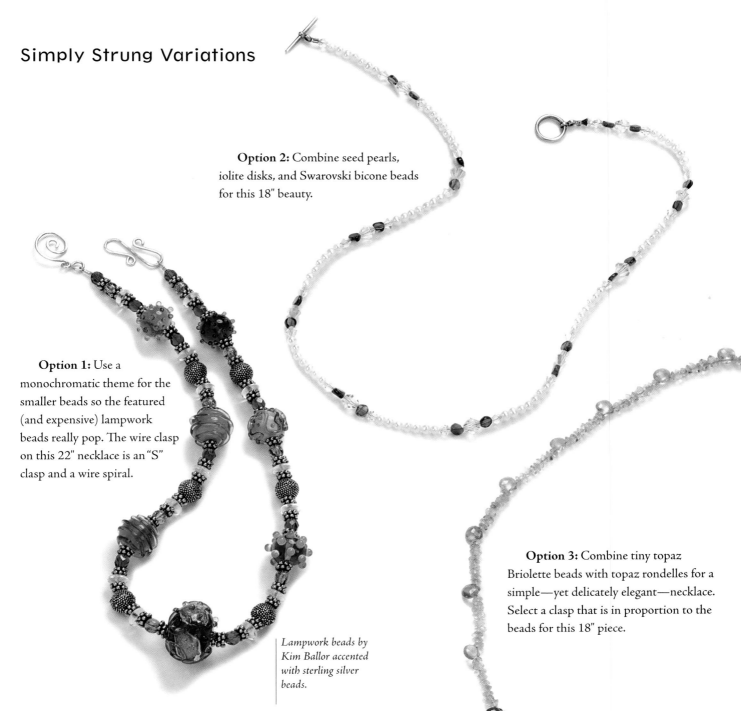

Option 2: Combine seed pearls, iolite disks, and Swarovski bicone beads for this 18" beauty.

Option 1: Use a monochromatic theme for the smaller beads so the featured (and expensive) lampwork beads really pop. The wire clasp on this 22" necklace is an "S" clasp and a wire spiral.

Lampwork beads by Kim Ballor accented with sterling silver beads.

Option 3: Combine tiny topaz Briolette beads with topaz rondelles for a simple—yet delicately elegant—necklace. Select a clasp that is in proportion to the beads for this 18" piece.

Multi-Strand Necklace

Sometimes a burst of color created by a number of colored strands of beads is the way to go. While there's no limit to the number of strands you can add, when using multiple strands, you'll need to keep weight and construction in mind as you arrange the beads. The bulk of this six-strand necklace may look heavy, but the amber chips are very light, making this necklace comfortable to wear for long periods.

Materials

3 to 8 strands amber chips

20 to 40 antique goldtone 2mm or 3mm metal beads ?

18-gauge gunmetal-coated copper Artistic Wire

Lightweight metal-core stringing cord

12 gold 2mm crimp beads

Wire cutters

Round nose pliers

Needle nose pliers

Flat file

Ruler

Bead board

Finished size: 18"

Instructions

1. Use wire to create a hook clasp, as shown on page 37, and put a large wrapped loop on one end, referring to instructions on page 35, if necessary.

2. Create a double wrapped loop with a large loop on one end. The loops need to be large to accommodate the number of strands that will be connecting.

3. Cut a 22" length of stringing cord.

4. Attach one end of the stringing cord to the double wrapped loop, using a crimp bead.

5. Add amber chips and small metal beads in a random manner, to fill 17" of stringing cord.

6. Attach the other end to the hook clasp with a crimp bead.

7. Repeat steps 3 through 6 five more times, making sure that the small metal beads fall in different places as you attach the strands to the clasps.

Seafoam Blues Necklace Variation

These are the same beads as in the Seafoam Blues Necklace, but they have been soaked in etching solution.

Two-Strand Seafoam Blues Necklace

The calm blue colors are so soothing in this 20" necklace. I always think of the beach when I see these beads. Kim Ballor created the lampwork beads, which are accented with Halcraft USA's aqua bead mix.

Three-Strand Jet Lariat

Lariats can be worn multiple ways: looped, tied, or knotted. This particular necklace features Halcraft USA Jet small bead mix. A lariat is a traditional jewelry style that goes in and out of style regularly. I like them because they can be worn several different ways, giving you many options.

Materials

100 to 150 assorted sizes and shapes Jet beads

Lightweight metal-core stringing cord

6 silver 2mm crimp beads

8 sterling silver 18-gauge jump rings

Wire cutters

Crimping pliers

Ruler

Bead tray

Finished size: 38"

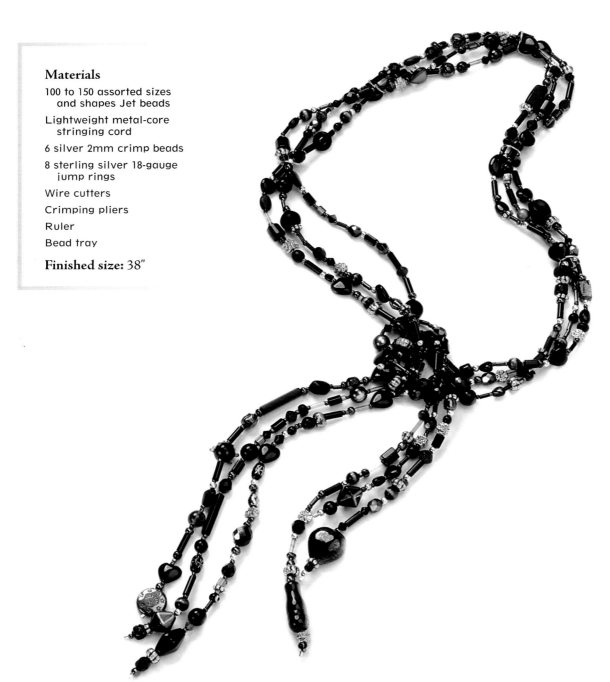

Instructions

1. Cut a 39" length of stringing cord.

2. Add a crimp bead to one end of the stringing cord, as instructed on page 60.

3. Cut off any excess stringing cord extending past the end of the crimp.

4. Add a small bead, followed by a large bead, and continue adding Jet beads, making sure to vary the sizes and shapes of the beads. Fill up the stringing cord with beads, and end with a large bead, followed by a small bead.

5. Add the second crimp bead and cut off any excess cord.

6. Repeat steps 1 through 5 two more times to create the other strands of the lariat.

7. Place all three strands on your work surface, aligning the ends.

8. Place a jump ring around all three strands in the center of the strands.

9. Add another jump ring about 6" to the left of the center and then a third jump ring 6" to the right of center.

10. Add another jump ring to each side at another 6" interval.

11. Place the lariat around your neck with the ends in front. Loosely begin to tie a square knot to wear.

Multi-Strand Fairy Necklace

This four-strand necklace and beaded tassel showcases the intricate lampwork figure by Sylvie Elise Lansdowne. When using an elaborate focal bead, keep the base of the necklace very simple. The multiple strands offer movement without distracting from the focal bead.

Materials

30 to 40 purple bugles

30 to 40 purple bicones

30 to 40 purple rondelles

30 to 40 purple disks

30 to 40 purple teardrops

30 to 40 purple small round beads

Focal bead

8 small lampwork beads

Lightweight metal-core stringing cord

10 gold 2mm crimp beads

20-gauge half-hard gold-filled wire

Wire cutters

Round nose pliers

Needle nose pliers

Crimping pliers

Flat file

Ruler

Bead tray

Clear tape

Instructions

To embellish the focal bead:

1. Use wire to create a hook clasp and double wrapped loop, as instructed on pages 37 and 35, respectively.

2. Cut an 8" length of wire and file the ends.

3. Put a wrapped loop on one end of the wire.

4. Add a bicone bead and the focal bead.

5. Put a small loop on the other end. Reserve one of the small lampwork beads to include in the tassel.

To make the strands:

1. Cut a 30" length of stringing cord.

2. Arrange small beads on the bead tray, varying the size and shape to fill 22" of cord. Fold a piece of clear tape around the end to keep beads from sliding off.

3. Slide 11" of the beads onto the cord and add the focal bead.

4. Add the other 11" of beads and bind the other end with tape.

5. Repeat steps 1 and 2, making sure that the beads complement the first strung cord. Bind one end with clear tape.

6. Slide on 11" of beads and then thread the end of the cord through the wrapped loop on the focal bead.

7. Add the other 11" of beads and bind the other end with tape. Also tape both ends of the first two cords to the work surface parallel to each other.

8. Repeat steps 5 through 7, except that before stringing through the wrapped loop of the focal bead, weave this third cord over and under the first two a couple of times and then through the focal bead.

9. Repeat step 8 for the fourth cord.

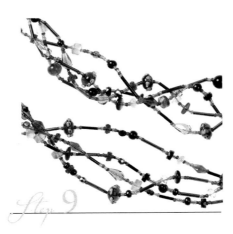

Step 9

10. Untape all four ends of one side from the work surface and insert these ends through a small round bead with a larger hole, then through a crimp, through one side of the clasp, and back through the crimp bead and the small round bead.

11. Snug the beads up to the clasp and crush crimp with the crimping pliers.

12. Repeat steps 10 and 11 on the other side.

Step 12

To create the tassel:

1. Cut four stringing cords into the following lengths: 12", 11", 10" and 9".

2. Insert one end of the 12" cord through the small lampwork bead, through the wire loop on the bottom of the focal bead, and back through the lampwork bead, so the cord is centered on the wire and both ends are even. Repeat this step with the three remaining cords.

3. Fill one of the cords with small beads, making sure the first bead is a bugle bead. Fill the cord except for 2" at the end.

4. Add a crimp bead to the end and close it with the crimping pliers.

5. Cut off any excess cord with the wire cutters.

6. Repeat steps 3 through 5 with the other cords.

Gallery

Autumn Dreams Choker

*The rusty tones of the faceted topaz rondelles in this 19"
piece I created complement the colors in Karen Ovington's
lampwork glass bead perfectly. To complete the piece, use a
barrel-shaped focal bead and a silver clasp.*

Asian-Themed Necklace with Detachable Pendant

*The two light-colored beads are carved olive wood and are beautiful on their own in this
20" piece. I wanted to be able to create a necklace that could be worn in more than one
way and this carved pendant has a wire hook so it can be removed.*

Just Make a Wish Necklace

This 22" necklace always puts me in a good mood. The whimsical colors selected by Kim Ballor for the lampwork beads and dragonfly are fun. Bali silver beads, toggle clasp, and 20-gauge sterling silver wire round out the materials needed to make this precious piece.

One-of-a-Kind Necklace

I took a class from Donna Milliron, who made the focal bead in this 22" necklace. In her glass bead-making technique, she breaks the mold to release the bead. The mysterious colors in the focal bead and its unusual shape, coupled with assorted black beads, bugle beads, fire-polished bicone beads, miracle beads, and irradiated pearls, makes for an intriguing piece.

Three-Strand Wire Necklace

This necklace by Louise Duhamel incorporates three graduated strands. Each strand grows longer in length, and then meets and converges, where they are finished with a length of jump rings and a handmade clasp. As the necklace flows with its semiprecious stones and glass and silver beads, charms are attached at unexpected intervals to dangle and attract.

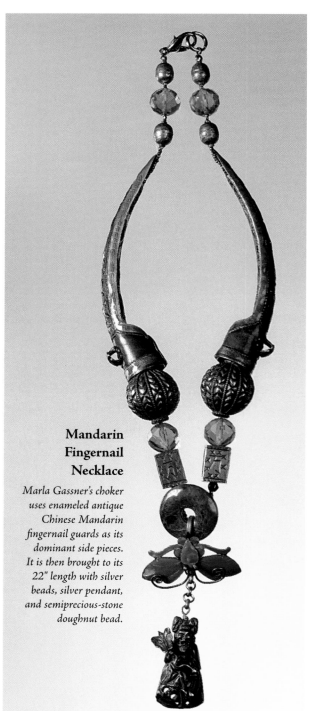

Mandarin Fingernail Necklace

Marla Gassner's choker uses enameled antique Chinese Mandarin fingernail guards as its dominant side pieces. It is then brought to its 22" length with silver beads, silver pendant, and semiprecious-stone doughnut bead.

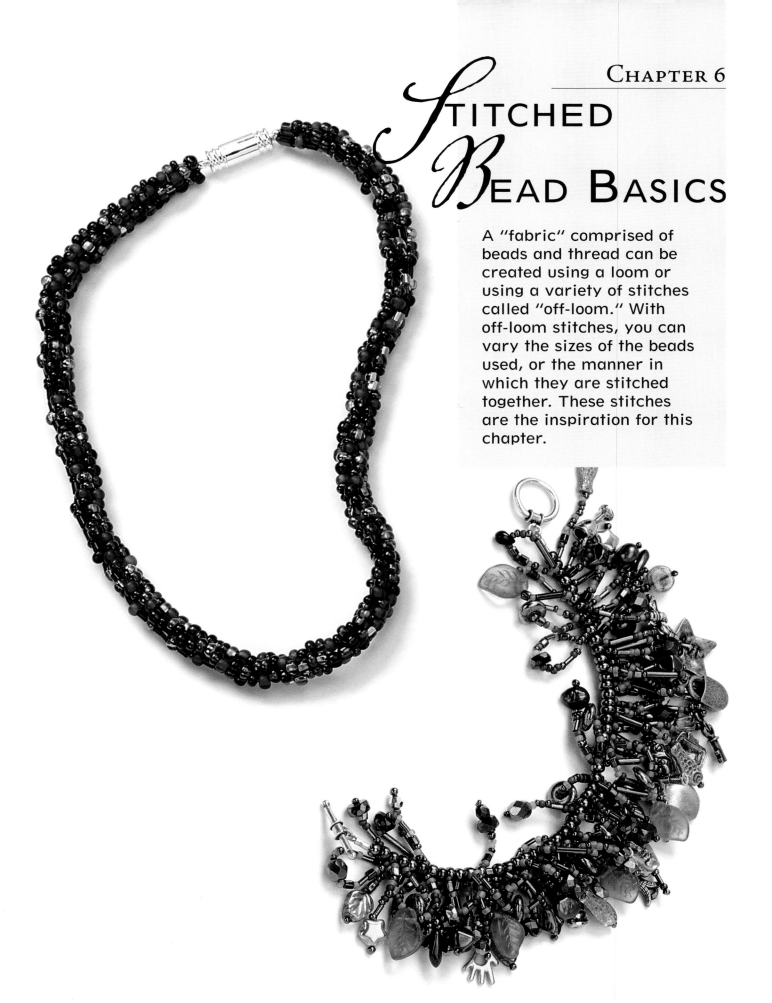

CHAPTER 6

Stitched
Bead Basics

A "fabric" comprised of
beads and thread can be
created using a loom or
using a variety of stitches
called "off-loom." With
off-loom stitches, you can
vary the sizes of the beads
used, or the manner in
which they are stitched
together. These stitches
are the inspiration for this
chapter.

Getting Started

For ease in learning off-loom stitches, beginners should consider using Japanese seed beads because of their uniformity of size and shape. Using these beads is much easier, as they will interlock smoothly and will not shift around.

I recommend using size 12 beading needles and size "B" Nymo beading threads. To start, thread the needle with a doubled length of thread and run the thread over beeswax or thread conditioner to strengthen the thread.

Experiment to see how tightl to pull the beads. I pull my beads very tightly together, and the resulting beadwork is very structural, since the beads do not shift very much due to the tightness of the thread. Other bead artists maintain a looser tension, and achieve a silky fabric feel to their beadwork.

The most important guide is to be consistent, regardless of how tightly you pull the beads. The shifts in tightness of the threads will be noticeable if you do not maintain consistency.

"Tension" Beads

When starting any stitched bead project, you'll need to add a "keeper" bead or "tension" bead to your thread to keep your beads from sliding off as you start. This bead will be removed later after the first few rows of beadwork are established.

The purpose of the tension bead is to help keep the beads on the thread and allow you to stitch the first couple of rows of beads together without the beads being too loose.

Contrary to how their name may sound, these beads are not like worry beads!

To add a tension bead:

1. Pass through a bead with your needle and move the bead down toward the end of the thread, leaving a 6" tail on the thread.

2. Pass through the bead again from the same direction.

3. Pull on the tail of the thread to tighten the thread around the bead.

4. After you have stitched four or five rows onto the beadwork, use the tip of your needle first to loosen the thread that is through the tension bead and then to pull the thread out of the hole. Remove the tension bead.

5. Thread the needle with both thread tails, if possible, and stitch the tails into the beadwork. You may need to stitch them in one at a time.

Most bead artists do not use knots to start or end threads. The knots are difficult to hide in the beadwork and are unattractive to see. The bulk of the knots also fill up the hole of the beads, making it difficult to stitch through a bead several times. This is a particular concern when creating a complicated piece which requires stitching through beads many times—sometimes as many as five or six times.

Ending a Thread

Stop stiching when you have about 6" or 7" left. This you enough length to pass through several beads.

It is always easier to end a thread with more thread length than you need, rather than too little.

1. Pass through several beads on the edge of the beadwork, bringing the needle out of an up bead.

4. Stitch down through a couple more edge beads and add another half-hitch knot. Repeat this step for a third half-hitch knot.

2. Begin to pull the thread through the bead, but stop when there is about a 2" diameter loop. Insert the needle through the loop.

5. Pull the thread taut and clip the excess with your wire cutters as close to the beadwork as possible. By pulling the thread taut, the end of the thread will disappear in between the beads.

3. Pull the needle and thread so the loop tightens up and the half-hitch knot created slips up and into the beadwork. You can help the loop move along with the tip of your needle.

Peyote stitching is the foundation for the Pleated Pods Peyote Necklace, shown at right and with detailed instructions on pages 107-110.

Adding a New Thread

More often then not, the initial thread length is not going to be enough to finish your stitched piece. In such cases, you will need to add in a new thread to continue your stitching.

Here's how:

1. Re-thread your needle and condition the thread.

2. Pass through several beads in the area where you stopped stitching, and work your way to the spot where the next bead will be added. The more zigs and zags you add, the more secure your thread anchor is going to be.

3. Pull on the excess thread tail that may be sticking out of the first bead you entered and cut it off very close to the beadwork.

Practicing with a Swatch

I find it's best to start out any project by stitching a small swatch of the beads I plan to use. It's a good way to evaluate how the beads will look together.

It's easy to skip making a swatch and get right to stitching on the project, but stitching a sample swatch is a good habit to maintain, so as not to be surprised or disappointed with your finished piece. Often, I'll turn the swatch into a bead or decorative element on another project.

Another benefit of creating a swatch is that you will be able to test how many times a bead can be stitched through without breaking it. It's far better to discover this information in a small swatch than in the middle of your beaded piece.

Variety of stitched peyote swatches.

The wire base supports Kristan Childs' numerous lampwork beads in this necklace. Improvisational beadwork effectively conceals much of the wire construction. As with any project involving thread, breakage can occur when the holes of the beads are full with thread, making it necessary for you to tug on the needle and thread to get it through a full bead. If a break does occur, simply follow the suggestions provided below.

Solving Challenges: Broken Threads and Beads

Inevitably, something will happen while stitching beads together on a project. A thread might break while you're pulling it through a bead for the fourth time, or the bead itself might break or chip. While frustrating, the challenge is to solve the problem so the error cannot be detected in the finished beadwork.

Dealing with a Broken Thread

1. When a thread breaks, leave the tail end where it is and do not cut it off right away.

2. Thread your needle and condition the new thread.

3. Anchor the new thread in the beadwork near where the broken thread is coming out of a bead. Stitch through the beads so the needle exits a bead near where the broken thread is sticking out.

4. Hold onto the broken thread with your other hand, so it can't pull back into the beadwork. Work your needle through the beadwork and through the same bead that has the broken thread. If you can pass through that bead, be sure to stitch through several of the beads that would have been added before and after the bead where the thread broke.

5. Use the tip of the needle to try to unthread the broken thread from the last few beads it had been stitched through, so you have a longer tail to use. Try to unthread the broken thread from enough beads so you have about 4" to 6" of thread.

Tip:
When passing through the beads around the broken thread, anchor these beads as much as possible, which eliminates the possibility of the broken thread working its way loose and the beads coming off. You must strengthen this area so it will not be weak when subjected to the wear and tear of being worn.

6. If you can get a length of thread loose from the beadwork, trim the frayed end with scissors and thread it onto a needle.

7. Take several zigzag stitches through the surrounding beads just as if you were ending a thread. Make sure that you are working with the beaded fabric so your stitches are hidden by the beads.

8. Cut off the excess original thread after four or five stitches and then go back to using the repair thread to continue your stitching.

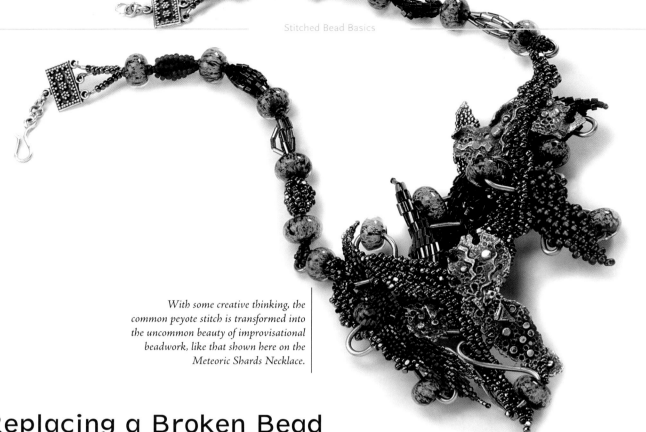

With some creative thinking, the common peyote stitch is transformed into the uncommon beauty of improvisational beadwork, like that shown here on the Meteoric Shards Necklace.

Replacing a Broken Bead

1. When a bead breaks, first check to see if any threads were broken when the bead broke. If threads also were broken, be sure to needle through the beads in the area to ensure they are secure before replacing the bead.

2. Select a bead that matches the bead that broke. If you are using beads that vary in size somewhat, try to use a bead that is slightly smaller than the original bead, as it will easily fit in the hole left by the broken bead.

3. Remove any remnants of the broken bead.

4. Thread a new needle and anchor the thread in the surrounding beadwork.

5. Hold the new bead in position in the hole left by the broken bead and use the tip of your needle to move any threads that had been stitched through the original bead to one side of the new bead.

6. Stitch through the new bead, pass through some of the surrounding beads to anchor the thread, and then pass back through the new bead from the other direction.

7. As you come out the other side of the new bead, loop the thread around the original threads and pass through the bead that is on the diagonal to the new bead. By stitching on the diagonal, you will begin to pull the threads off to the side, allowing the new bead to sit properly in the stitched piece.

8. If necessary, pass through neighboring beads and try to loop around the original threads and anchor them on the diagonal from the opposite direction.

9. If you can, pass through the new bead several times; by filling it with thread, you will be working it into the fabric of the surrounding beadwork and the repair will be less noticeable.

If you are creating a sculptural piece with a lot of texture and dimension, the repaired spot will be a great area to strategically place some embellishment if you are unable to repair the beadwork without any evidence remaining.

I keep brush-on white correction fluid in my tool box for these types of repairs. When I'm about to work on a repair, I'll dot a little of the correction fluid on the beads around the repair spot. Then, when I'm starting to embellish the bead fabric, the white dots are a reminder to see if I need to add some embellishment. Once the correction fluid is dry, it can be easily scraped off with the tip of your needle or fingernail, and no one will ever be the wiser!

Learning Off-Loom Stitches

In all cases, use beeswax or thread conditioner on the thread. For most stitches, I use a doubled thread, as this helps to quickly fill up the bead holes and creates a strong bead fabric..

Basic Peyote (Gourd) Stitch

Peyote is one of the most-used stitches in creating beaded fabric. It is easy to stitch and can be modified in many ways for a variety of different looks.

1. Add a tension bead length of doubled thread, leaving a 6" tail.

2. String on 11 more beads.

> The first couple of rows in peyote beadwork are the most difficult rows to stitch when starting a new project.

3. Bring the needle around the last bead and pass through the third bead. The last two beads added will sit on top of each other. You may need to use your fingers or the tip of your needle to get these two beads into position.

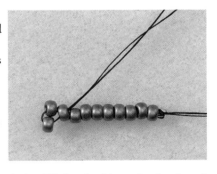

4. Add a bead, pass through the fifth bead, add another bead, and pass through the seventh bead. Continue adding beads in this manner to the end of the row. You should notice that there are "hills" and "valleys" (or up-beads and down-beads) created. You will stitch through the up-beads and the beads that are added sit in the valleys, and become the up-beads for the next row.

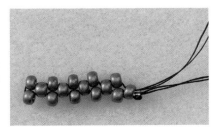

5. Turn the piece, string on a bead, and continuing adding beads in each of the valleys and passing through the up-beads until the swatch is almost square.

6. End the stitching thread in the piece using one of the techniques described on page 79.

7. Unthread the tension bead and thread the needle with the two tails. End this thread using the other ending technique, page 79.

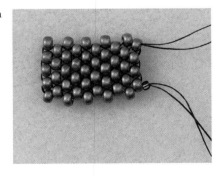

The smaller ivory beads are worked in double-peyote, while the larger blue beads are worked in the basic peyote.

Double-Peyote Stitch

In this variation, you add two beads at a time, but treat them as a set. You stitch through both beads, as if they were a single bead. They are counted as a single bead as well.

If you are planning a project that will combine beads of different sizes in a piece, consider using double-peyote stitch, so you have the choice of adding two smaller beads as a set in combination with a single larger bead. This technique works especially well if you are combining 11° beads and 8° beads.

1. Thread on a tension bead, and then add 12 beads (six two-bead sets).

2. Bring the needle around, add two beads, and pass through the fifth and sixth beads (the two beads in the third set).

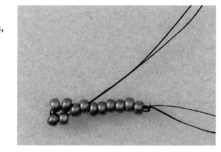

3. Continue adding two beads per set until you reach the end of the row.

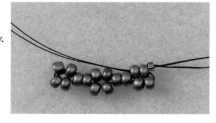

4. Turn the piece and add two beads at a time to build up the rows. At the end of the third row, it should be easy to see the hills and valleys created by the peyote stitch. You will add the sets of beads in the valleys and stitch through the hills, just as in the basic peyote.

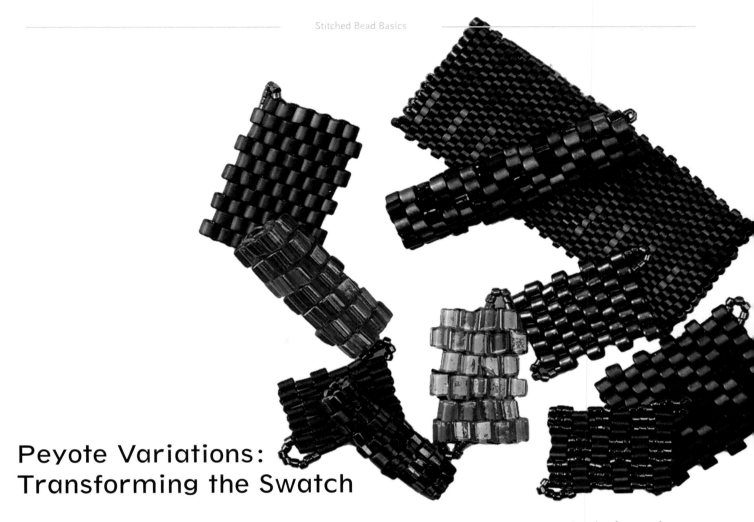

Samples of test swatches.

Peyote Variations: Transforming the Swatch

Adding loops to the swatch:

1. Once the swatch is to the desired size, needle through the beads until the needle is exiting a bead at the edge and end of a row.

2. Add six seed beads to the thread. (Size 11° beads work well for creating loops.)

3. Position the end of the six beads against the swatch and pass through a bead near the end of the row to anchor the loop. Pass through another bead in the row, and then pass back through the smaller beads again to strengthen the loop.

4. Work the needle through the bead swatch (as if you were tying off) to the opposite corner.

5. Add a six-bead loop, as you did above, to this corner also. The more thread you can pass through the beads and the loops, the stronger the swatch will be.

6. End the cord by knotting around threads within the swatch, as explained in the Ending a Thread section, page 79.

7. Pass through two or three beads and knot a second time as the loops on swatches often are subjected to a lot of wear and tear.

8. Cut off the excess thread and remove the tension bead.

9. Thread the needle onto the tails and work the tails into the swatch, ending by knotting around threads. Pull taut and cut off the excess thread.

Turning the looped swatch into a bead segment:

This finished bead segment can become a dangle for an earring, a dangle to hang off a clasp on a necklace, or a segment in a necklace or bracelet project.

1. Cut a 5" length of wire.

2. Put a wrapped loop on one end, as detailed on page 35, and a small seed bead that coordinates with the beads in the swatch.

3. Slide one loop of the swatch onto wire.

4. Add enough beads to cover the diagonal length of swatch. These can be seed beads or even more decorative beads.

5. Slip the other end of the wire through the other loop on the swatch.

6. Finish segment with a flat coil or square coil, as instructed on page 39, or another wrapped loop.

Zipping the swatch into a bead:

Be sure the hills and valleys that form the edges of the swatch will fit together and interlock before you stop stitching additional rows. If they don't line up, add one more row of beads and check again.

1. Pass through the beads until the thread is coming out of a bead at the end of a row on the edge of the swatch.

2. Use your fingertips to bend the edges of the swatch together.

3. Begin stitching the sides of the swatch together, passing through a bead from each side for each stitch as you go, just like closing a zipper.

This bracelet below evolved from a basic strip of peyote. The extreme texture was accomplished in two phases, as the piece was completed and then additional width and dimension were added a year later.

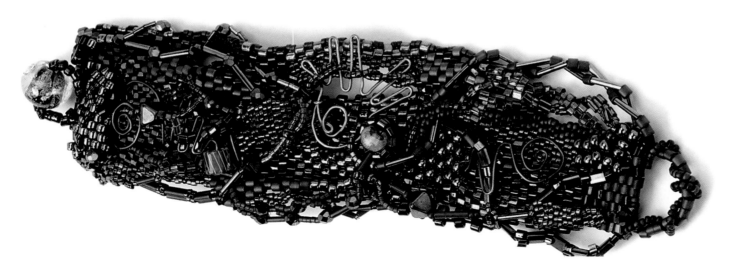

Tubular Peyote Stitch

In addition to stitching a flat band and then zipping up the edges, you can start out stitching beads in the round using the peyote stitch. The number of beads added to the starting row determines the diameter of the tube. Shorter base rows create narrow tubes, while longer rows—even up to 50 beads or more—result in a tube that then can be transformed into an amulet bag or small evening purse that can hold a tube of lipstick. All you'll need to do is stitch the bottom together and add a hanging strap.

Although the instructions here use basic peyote to complete the tube, you can also use double-peyote and triple-peyote stitches. In doing so, be extremely careful when counting the beads for the first row and stitching the first couple of rows to create the hills and valleys.

1. Add a tension bead and the number of beads required to make a ring the diameter you want.

2. Pass thread through the beads again, skipping the tension bead.

3. Remove the tension bead and tie a square knot to secure the threads.

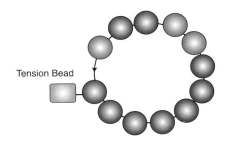

Tension Bead

In regard to step 3, make sure you leave nearly two beads' width of slack in the thread going through the beads to accommodate the movement of the beads during the stitching. You'll work the tail in later.

4. Pass through the first bead to the right of the knot. Gently tug the beads around on the thread ring so they slide a bit and the knot is hidden inside a bead.

5. Add a bead to the thread, skip the next bead, and pass through the third bead from the knot. Continue adding and skipping beads to create the first row with hills and valleys, just like in basic peyote. Be sure to stitch around the ring in the same direction, especially after adding a new thread.

● To support your beadwork, cut a toilet paper tube lengthwise and slip the base ring over the tube. The cut in the tube will allow the beadwork to determine the diameter. The tube will support your beadwork, making it easier to stitch through the beads and to view how the work is progressing. If you really want to make the beadwork stable, once the base ring is slipped onto the tube, use clear tape to tape the top and bottom edges together so they do not shift.

● If your tube has an even number of beads in the row, you will need to go through two beads at the end of each row (you will stitch through the two beads on the diagonal which is also called stepping up). If you have an odd number of beads you will just keep stitching and will start a new row. With an odd number of beads in tubular peyote, you are essentially stitching one extremely long row around and around until the tube has reached the desired length.

This simple "tennis" style bracelet was stitched using "E" beads. It is a quick project, similar to the Zipped Peyote Choker (shown above and detailed on pages 94 and 95), that is easy to vary the look by changing the beads.

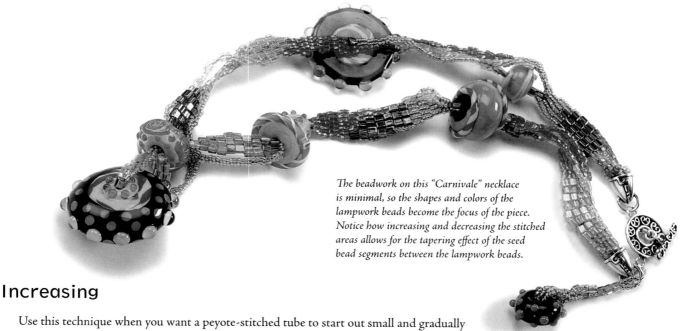

The beadwork on this "Carnivale" necklace is minimal, so the shapes and colors of the lampwork beads become the focus of the piece. Notice how increasing and decreasing the stitched areas allows for the tapering effect of the seed bead segments between the lampwork beads.

Increasing

Use this technique when you want a peyote-stitched tube to start out small and gradually flare out into a larger diameter.

1. Add two beads in the place of one bead, as shown in Figure I-1, wherever you want to increase the diameter of the project.

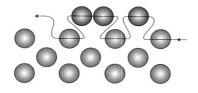

Figure I-1

2. The next time around the tube, stitch through the first bead, add a bead, and then stitch through the second bead, as shown.

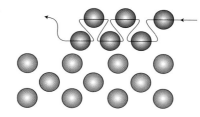

Figure I-2

Decreasing

At the end of a project, you may wish to make the tube taper down to a smaller diameter. This is attractive when attaching a clasp, and will make your work look more graceful.

1. Pass through two beads without adding a bead, as in Figure D-1.

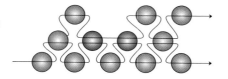

Figure D-1

2. Pull the thread tight.

3. In the next row, add only one bead (a larger bead, if possible) in the spot where the two beads are located, as shown.

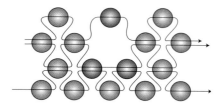

Figure D-2

I find it easier to start out stitching the piece at the diameter that most of the beadwork will be stitched and then adding the increases or decreases afterwards on the ends. This is especially helpful if your project is primarily a tube and you don't plan for it to increase and decrease other than on the ends.

Brick Stitch

Another popular stitch used in creating off-loom beaded pieces, the finished brick stitch does look very similar to peyote stitch, but the construction techniques are completely different.

As with peyote stitch, the brick stitch is easier to learn using the cylinder shapes of the Japanese seed beads than rounded seed beads, as the beads will nestle together and interlock.

1. Because you do not need a tension bead in this stitch, begin by cutting a length of stringing material, threading a needle and conditioning the thread.

2. Pass through two beads, leaving a 6" tail, and then pass through both beads again, stitching in the same direction. Use your fingers to position the beads so they are side by side and hold them so the thread is coming down through the second bead.

3. Add a bead and pass through the second bead from the top down, as shown in Figure B-1.

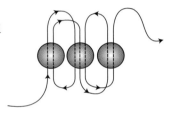

Figure B-1

4. Add a bead and pass through the third bead from the bottom up.

5. Continue adding beads, repeating steps 3 and 4 as in Figure B-2, until the base row is the desired length.

Figure B-2

6. Once the base row is created, stitch back through the row, in a zigzag (up and down) manner until you are back to the beginning of the row. This strengthens the base row and will make it more stable to handle.

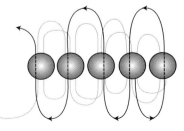

Figure B-3

7. Notice that there are threads connecting the beads across the top and the bottom of the base row. These threads will be stitched under when attaching the additional rows.

8. Add two beads at the start of each new row. Adding two beads allows you to create beadwork where there is no thread showing on the ends, so your beadwork will look more attractive and professional.

9. Referring to Figure B-4, pass the needle under the threads between the second and third bead from back to front (the needle slides under the threads to anchor the beads). Pull the thread tight and then pass through the second bead you just added on the second row from the bottom to the top.

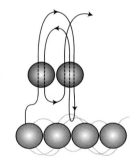

Figure B-4

10. Add another bead, pass the needle under the threads between the third and fourth bead from back to front, pull the thread tight, and pass through the new bead from the bottom up, as shown in Figure B-5. Continue adding beads in this manner until you reach the end of the row.

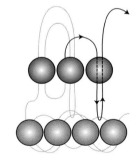

Figure B-5

11. Flip the beadwork piece around horizontally and work the next row from left to right, starting by adding two beads for the next row.

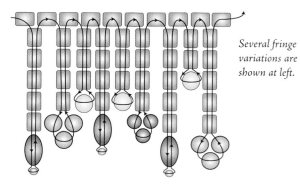

Embellishing Your Beadwork

One of the most enjoyable parts of creating a project is adding the embellishments. Fringe is a popular way to add color, texture, and movement to beadwork. After you've created the base, experiment with adding a variety of styles of fringe. Fringe doesn't have to be all one length to be attractive; it can be longer in the center than on the sides for a "V" look. Or, it can taper down getting longer and longer toward the left or right side of a piece. Even a random look to fringe, combining many different lengths and styles will add visual interest.

Basic Fringe

Basic fringe adds movement, texture, and dimension to your beadwork. This type of fringe is the most simple to create.

1. Begin by adding several beads onto the thread. Put a small bead on the end and pass back through the beads that were just added. The end bead is called a "pivot" bead, because you use this bead as a pivot point to stitch back up the fringe.

2. Pull the thread so the beads are snug, but not too tight, and standing at attention. The little bit of slack will allow the beads to lie naturally. It may take a little practice to get the feel. If the beads are too tight, you can insert the tip of your needle into the loop of the thread at the pivot bead and wiggle the thread looser.

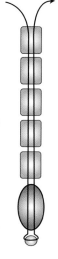

Putting a half-hitch at the base of each fringe to anchor the fringe is a good habit to get into, because if the thread breaks, only the beads on that particular fringe will come off. If you don't put a knot or a half-hitch between each fringe, you may loose all of the beads on all of the fringes. To make a half-hitch, wrap the thread around the base, but do not pull it tight, leaving a loop. Then, pass through the loop with the needle and pull the loop tight to anchor the thread.

Fringe Variations

Fringe with a Loop

Using fringe with a loop highlights a small bead, which can add sparkle or a new element.

1. Slide several beads onto the thread.

2. Put three small beads on the end and pass back up through the beads last added before the five beads were added.

3. Pull the bead thread snugly to create a loop out of the three beads.

Fringe with a Dangle

Fringe with a dangle is very similar in style to the fringe with a loop and is a good way to add charms and other embellishments to your piece.

1. Slide several beads onto the thread.

2. Add three small beads, followed by a metal charm, and then three more small beads.

3. Pass back up through the beads that were first added.

4. Pull the bead thread so the beads are snug, but not tight.

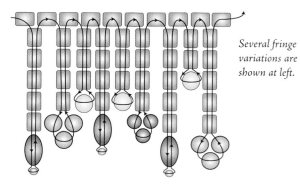

Several fringe variations are shown at left.

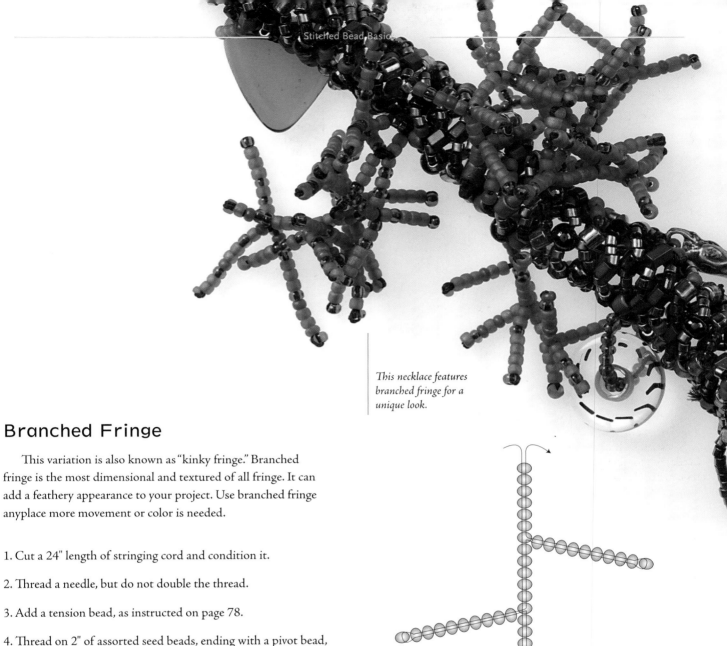

This necklace features branched fringe for a unique look.

Note the thread path necessary for creating branched fringe.

Branched Fringe

This variation is also known as "kinky fringe." Branched fringe is the most dimensional and textured of all fringe. It can add a feathery appearance to your project. Use branched fringe anyplace more movement or color is needed.

1. Cut a 24" length of stringing cord and condition it.

2. Thread a needle, but do not double the thread.

3. Add a tension bead, as instructed on page 78.

4. Thread on 2" of assorted seed beads, ending with a pivot bead, and pass back through the last four beads added. Pull the thread tight.

5. Come out the side of the fringe and add six seed beads (the last bead is the pivot bead).

6. Pass back through the five added beads to complete one branch of the kinky fringe.

7. Pass back through four of the original beads and add a short branch.

8. Pass back through five of the original beads and add a long branch.

9. Continue adding branches of varying length until you get back to the top.

Even your branches can sprout branches of their own for a thick and fluffy look!

91

Fringed Party Bracelet

This bracelet is pure fun to wear. You won't be able to stop playing with it! And the real fun is that it only looks complicated, as it is made with a variety of fringe styles. You can coordinate the bead colors with the small decorative glass beads or include a wide variety of colors, finishes, and sizes for a riot of color.

Materials

3 to 4 oz. "E" beads

30 to 40 oz. small decorative glass beads

8 to 10 small metal charms

12" medium-weight metal-core stringing cord

Nylon beading thread

Toggle-style clasp

4 tube-style crimp beads

Clear fingernail polish

#12 beading needle

Thread conditioner

Beeswax

Scissors

Wire cutters

Crimping pliers

Ruler

Bead tray

Finished size: 7½"

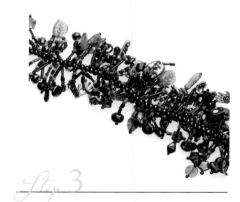

Instructions

To create the base bracelet:

1. Use the crimp bead to attach one half of the clasp to one end of the stringing cord, referring to the instructions on page 60, if necessary.

2. Add enough "E" beads to encircle wrist plus ½" more.

3. Put the crimp bead on the other end and add the other side of the clasp, making sure to leave enough slack on the stringing to hold the equivalent of three beads. This space will be taken up with the fringe.

To anchor the thread:

1. Thread the needle with approximately 36" of beading thread and condition the thread.

2. Start about four beads from one end of the base bracelet and insert the needle through the last three beads, making sure not to go through the end bead. Pull thread through the three beads and stop when the thread tails just disappear into the fourth bead.

3. Tie a half-hitch knot around the stringing cord by wrapping the thread around the cord and passing the needle through the loop before pulling it tight.

4. Dip the tip of the needle into clear nail polish and swipe polish onto the knot to securely seal it. Wait a few seconds for the polish to set. Use this method to begin and end threads.

Tip

The clear fingernail polish seals the half-hitches so they will not work loose if a thread breaks on a fringe.

To finish:

1. Fill the length of the bracelet with fringes, as instructed on pages 90-91. Vary the length and style of the fringes. Be sure to add charms to a few of the fringe, but try to space them out so there's approximately one charm for each ½" in length.

2. Add a second row of fringe to create a full bracelet.

3. A third layer of fringe gets challenging in threading through the base row of beads, but will be very fluffy and full. If you find a bead that you can't get the needle through, try to pass through a bead that is in the base of a nearby fringe. With three rows of fringes, it'll be nearly impossible to see the base row.

Step 1

Step 3

Zipped Peyote Choker

Depending on the materials used, this simple choker can be elegant or casual. Attractive at a variety of lengths, this style of necklace is easily embellished with a single focal bead as a pendant or with many beads.

Materials

8 to 10 oz. seed beads in
   coordinating colors and sizes

Nylon beading thread

Magnetic clasp

#12 beading needle

Thread conditioner

Scissors

Ruler

Finished size: 18"

Instructions

1. Thread needle, double it, and condition thread.

2. Add a tension bead, as instructed on page 78.

3. Add enough "E" beads to fill 17½".

4. Add a bead and begin to stitch back down the row using basic peyote stitch, referring to the stitch instructions on page 83, if necessary.

5. Continue stitching until you have added eight more rows of beads. If you want the diameter of your choker to be larger, add more rows.

6. Use your fingertips to begin to roll the two outside edges of the peyote-stitched band toward each other. (Wrapping the beadwork around a pencil may help.) Align the ends and continue aligning the hills and valleys of the edges.

7. Insert the needle in the end bead and begin stitching up the edges, moving from one edge to the other to secure.

8. When you get to the end, hold the jump ring of the magnetic clasp against the end of the beadwork and stitch through the loop. Take several stitches, making sure to pass through all of the end beads in the tube. Be sure to stitch through the clasp finding enough times until you believe it will be secure and sustain the wear and tear of use.

9. Needle back down to the other end of the necklace and stitch through the other side of the clasp, attaching it to the beadwork.

When you feel you've added enough rows, check to see if the edges of the peyote-stitched band will interlock when stitched closed. If they don't, and you have "hills" matching "hills," add another row of peyote stitching. Leave your needle attached and coming out one of the end edge beads.

Variations:

- Add bands of peyote tubes in contrasting colors to embellish the base tube and to slide over and hide the clasp. That way, it won't matter which way the necklace hangs when worn.

- Attach fringe and other embellishments to the front of the necklace.

Gallery

Turquoise Fiber Fringe Bracelet

Kim Ballor's bracelet design features her own lampwork focal bead and is embellished with seed bead fringe and fibers. Additionally, a silver butterfly charm, sterling silver wire, fibers, and a Bali silver toggle clasp are needed to complete the 7½" piece.

Bead Encrusted Pin

Created by Bonnie Clewans, this 5" x 4" pin is embellished with new and vintage glass beads and Japanese seed beads placed on a vintage filigree frame.

Ruffled Cuff

This 7½" bracelet by Louise Duhamel was created after she took a class by mixed media artist Teresa Stoa. Somehow, Louise's bracelet had a mind of its own and as she says "was born through my mistakes!" With its seed beads, pearls, semiprecious stones, and button clasp, it expands first in length and breadth to create a netted cuff, before continuing with a multitude of loops that grow up and out, away from the base. The finished bracelet feels light and airy though its visual presence is on a much grander scale.

Stick Necklace

This little horn stick with its 25 holes lay on the floor of designer Marla Gassner's studio for several years. One day, this piece just flowed out of Marla as though "it had been waiting in a placenta to be born." With its horn stick, antique jade charms, and seed beads, it became the inspiration and centerpiece for her second book, Beyond the Bead and I.

The Shag Carpet of Pearls Bracelet

Kate McKinnon's 7½" piece is hand-sewn, using an adaptation of the square stitch. The pearls are individually wired and then included in the weave of the piece, which also includes Thai silver and Czech seed beads. Then, a fringed edge wrap is applied for strength and durability.

Industrial Chic Bracelet

This piece is hand-sewn using square stitch with an edge wrap that Kate McKinnon devised to add strength to sewn pieces. This bracelet is 7½" long and features Thai silver and Precious Metal Clay elements Kate created herself.

Short Fringe Bracelet

Tracia Williams' design with short colorful fringe highlights the rich colors of the lampwork artist Joe Worrell's beads in this fun 6" bracelet. Tracia used "E" beads, seed beads, cube beads, Bali silver spacers, and silver coil beads to create this look.

CHAPTER 7

SCULPTURAL BEADING

All of the techniques explored thus far contribute to a firm foundation for jewelry making. In this chapter, each of the key techniques—wirework, stringing, and basic bead stitching—will be combined in a variety of ways to complete a variety of projects. For the most part, the foundation of most of the projects starts with peyote stitch. Once the foundation is built with peyote stitch, we will take the piece to the next level, to create beadwork pieces using "improvisational" beadwork.

Preparing for Improvisational Beadwork

To start an improvisational beadwork piece, gather together a wide variety of materials on your work surface that all have the potential of being included in the project: the focal elements, such as lampwork focal beads and secondary beads; tubes of seed beads in coordinating colors and varying sizes; charms; findings; and clasp options.

Now, think about the finished piece you want to create. Think back to the earlier chapters where you were asked to go through your jewelry box to discover what you like and what you tend to prefer in jewelry.

Begin to arrange the focal beads on your work surface as you would like to see them featured in the finished piece. Now consider how these beads will be connected together. Will they be connected completely by beadwork? Will you include wire?

Think back to the questions in the earlier chapters on composition, balance, and proportion and keep these principles in mind when considering how the piece will be constructed.

When creating most stitched projects seen in this chapter, I recommend the following when starting out:

- Use Nymo "B" thread in a color that complements your beads.

- Use a #12 needle, double the thread, and condition it.

Creating Open Spaces and Texture

Adding dimension through positive and negative space is another way to achieve visual interest. Sometimes, a solid piece of beadwork is overwhelming to look at, as there is so much going on that your eye doesn't know where to go. Creating a piece with open spaces will add interest, but will not be so busy.

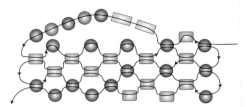

Adding Arches

Begin by adding arches to the beadwork. Here's how:

1. String on about 1" up to 2" of beads. These can be beads that match the beads on the edge of the beadwork or beads that will serve to introduce a new bead color, shape, or style.

2. With the beads strung on the thread, move the thread around to determine where to anchor the other end to the edge of the beadwork. Pass through the bead closest to where you wish to anchor the arch and continue stitching down the row of the beadwork.

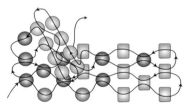

3. Add several arches using different types of beads.

4. Stitch back down the side where you just added the arch to begin to build up the arch. If you like, you can just stitch back and forth on the arch to build up that section. This is helpful when you don't want to increase the overall width of the project.

Creating Bridges

To create a **bridge**, you will do the same thing as adding an arch, only you will bring the loose end with the beads over onto the beadwork and anchor the bridge onto the middle portion of the beadwork, rather than just on an edge. The difference between the two terms for reference is that an arch occurs along the edge of the beadwork and a bridge crosses over and anchors on the middle of the beadwork.

You can also attach charms, lampwork beads, shells, and other interesting beads to the beadwork using arches and bridges. If desired, try adding decorative wire shapes to create interest

and texture. Attach the wire shapes to the beadwork by stitching through the wire shapes to create small beaded loops using seed beads.

Add lampwork beads to the piece with bridges or arches, making sure to place them throughout the piece. If desired, you can slide a bead onto the wire before shaping the wire into a segment. This will help integrate the wire into the beadwork.

Attaching the Beadwork to the Wire Frame

Once you have a stitched piece ready, you can securely attach the beadwork to a wire framework at the ends. Here's how:

1. Bead back and forth on the last 1" or so of the beadwork, building up the width.

2. Once it is wide enough to connect when wrapped around the wire framework, wrap the beadwork around the framework and stitch through the edge beads to zip up the last ½".

3. To lengthen the beaded tube in order to hide the wire wraps that might be on the wire framework, use the tubular peyote stitch, as instructed on page 87, to extend the beadwork. You may want to continue stitching beads onto the piece in order to build up the end of the beadwork since some width would be lost because of the wrapping around the end of the framework.

4. End the beadwork in the same manner for the other end of the bracelet to attach it to the hook portion of the wire framework. Be sure to bend and flex the bracelet, and try it on frequently.

Ask yourself the following questions:

- Is there a place on the project that looks skimpy and needs more beads?

- Is there a spot on the project where the beadwork is pulling away from the wire framework?

- Are there areas where the project looks too dense with one color and another color should be introduced via a bridge or arch?

- Is the bracelet wide enough? If not, do you want to add arches and open areas or do you want to build up the area with peyote stitch to create more beadwork fabric?

- Is the bracelet too wide? To solve this, could you fold over one of the edges onto the beadwork and stitch it down to anchor it? Or, could you put a pleat in the center of the beaded fabric to pull in the width?

Starting an Improvisational Peyote-Stitched Piece

Start out small! You don't need to invest time in developing a huge piece of beadwork when you're beginning. While this project is small, you'll be able to create a piece with great impact. Also, be sure to experiment with sizes and bead inclusions.

Gather the Materials

For any improvisational peyote-stitched piece, you will need the following:

- Japanese seed beads in several complementary colors in 11° and 8°
- Small faceted beads, such as bicones or rondelles
- Nymo "B" beading thread
- #12 beading needle
- Scissors
- Watercolor dish

Embellished peyote swatch in a Precious Metal Clay frame.

Adding dimension and texture to a peyote-stitched base creates visual interest. A peyote swatch is a nice project to start out with when experimenting with improvisational beadwork.

1. Using the 8° Japanese seed beads, create a peyote swatch that has 12 beads in the base row, as instructed on page 84. Make the swatch about 2" long.

2. Begin to embellish the swatch and pass through a few beads, bringing the needle out up in the middle of the swatch.

3. Add several seed beads to the thread in preparation for creating a bridge. You will want to slide the beads down to the base of the thread, and hold the thread just above the beads with your fingertips. Move the thread around to determine where you want them to be positioned.

4. Insert the needle into the bead swatch right where the last bead is so the seed beads sit on top of the beadwork in a row without any excess thread showing.

5. Needle through the swatch to anchor these beads and come back up at the end of the added beads. Determine if you're going to do single- or double-peyote stitch to add beads to the first row of seed beads and add another row.

6. Continue to randomly add beads to the surface of the swatch, changing color and direction. Perhaps you'd like to add another 11/0 seed bead bridge to go off in another direction.

7. Add a few slightly larger beads to the beaded surface for interest. Perhaps several seed beads could be used to make a loop. Then, stitch back through the beads and stitch the loop to the surface of the beadwork.

When the stitching is completed, think about what you would like to do with this swatch. You could add loops and use the swatch as a pendant on a chain. Perhaps you could stitch several swatches together to create a bracelet from the embellished swatches.

For the swatch in this project, I created a PMC frame, using the wooden block of a rubber stamp as the form, and attached the swatch to the inside of the frame using jewel glue. Small loops were stitched onto the back of the swatch to accommodate a chain or neck ring.

The finished swatch inserted into a PMC frame.

A Bracelet Study

This is one of my favorite projects, because depending on the types of lampwork beads used and the seed bead colors, you can create a wide range of looks. Leaving many open spaces can be as interesting as a dense section of beads.

Materials

5 to 7 small focal beads or a lampwork bead set

4 to 6 oz. of seven or eight colors and/or styles of seed beads with varying textures and finishes to complement your focal beads (Be sure to include seed beads in the following sizes: 11°, 8°, and 6°.)

2 to 3 oz. of bugle beads in complementary colors (Be sure to cull through the bugle beads to eliminate any broken ones or ones with sharp edges.)

36" sterling silver 20-gauge wire

Nymo "B" beading thread

#12 beading needle

Scissors

Wire cutters

Round nose pliers

Flat file

Watercolor dish

Finished size: 8"

Instructions

1. Thread the needle and condition the thread.

2. Add a tension bead, as instructed on page 78.

3. Start out by adding about 1" of each style/color of seed beads. If you have a wide variety of sizes, such as 11° seed beads and 6° beads, plan to stitch the 11° beads with double-peyote stitch. With this idea, you will want to add the 11° seed beads in sets of two beads.

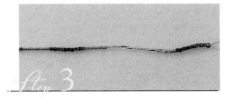

The 11° seed beads are added in pairs to be stitched in double-peyote stitch.

4. Fill the thread with enough beads to encircle your wrist plus about ½" of beads.

5. Begin to stitch the row, matching the beads as closely as possible. Stitch back and forth on this row, creating a strip of peyote-stitched beadwork that looks like small patches of beads joined together end to end.

6. After stitching the fourth row, begin to blend the beads into the adjoining patches. Stitch on a couple of the lighter beads to the edge of a darker patch and vice versa. The patches should seem to blend together.

Tips:

• Don't worry about the different bead sizes, it'll all work out.

To assemble the bracelet:

1. Weave the beaded strip in and out of a wire base to begin assembling the bracelet.

2. Create several wire segments (basically wire wiggles with rounded bends with the round nose pliers) using the 20-gauge sterling silver wire. Make sure to put a loop on each end to connect the segments. These loops do not need to be wrapped loops, since the beadwork will be attached to the wire and will prevent the loops from being pulled apart.

3. After bending the wire segments, join the segments together using the loops, to create a bracelet that would reach around your wrist, plus about 1" in length.

4. After joining the segments, add a simple hook clasp to one end, and a spiral to the other end, as detailed on pages 36 and 41, respectively.

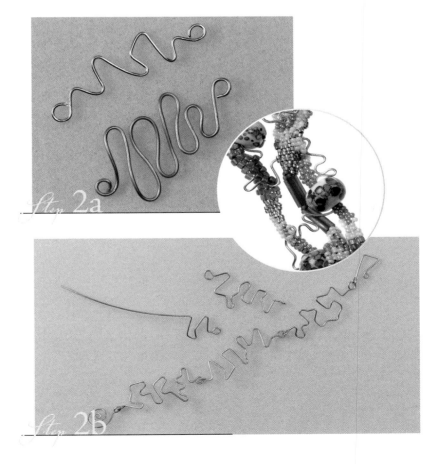

5. Loosely arrange the beaded peyote strip on the wire piece, weaving the strip in and out, and up and down through the wire. You can twist the beadwork to create texture if you like.

6. Continue stitching up and down the peyote strip and then begin to create arches, as instructed on page 101, that loop around the wire framework. You can also attach the beadwork to the wire with a loop and then reinforce the loop with peyote stitch.

7. At one end, stitch back and forth on the beadwork to widen the area.

8. When the end is wide enough, bend it around the wire framework at the base of the hook clasp and stitch the section closed, zipping the two sides together, referring to page 86 for assistance, if necessary. You may need to stitch down the length of the bracelet some to build up the width in proportion.

9. Repeat steps 7 and 8 for the other end of the clasp.

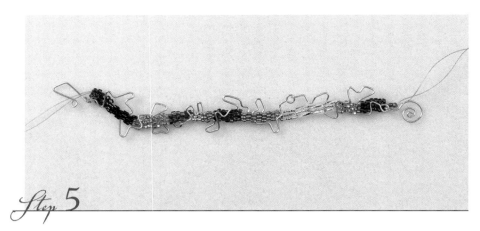

Step 5

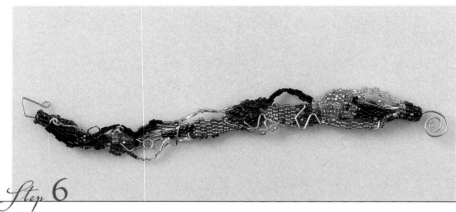

Step 6

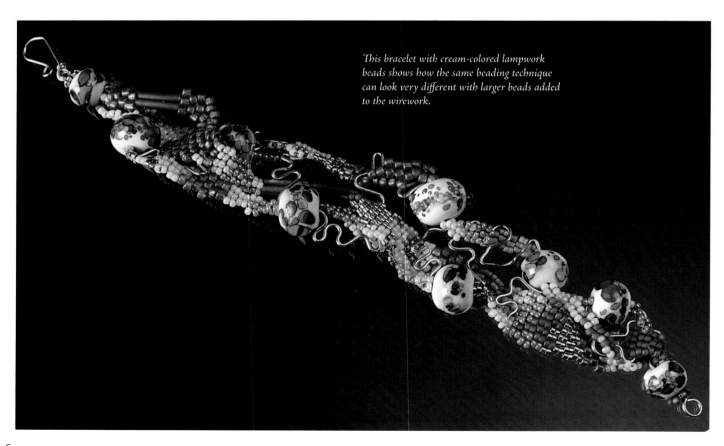

This bracelet with cream-colored lampwork beads shows how the same beading technique can look very different with larger beads added to the wirework.

Pleated Pods Peyote Necklace

The structure of this necklace developed entirely by accident. I wanted to create vertical segments that looked like they were growing together. I had put an extremely long arch between two of the segments that just didn't look right, and the amount of open space was causing the beadwork to sag. In an attempt to fix it, I pinched up the edges of beaded fabric along the arch and on the back, I zipped the beads together to create an invisible seam. This made the edges of the arch pucker. I really liked the effect and continued adding openings and pleats. Some of the pleats were left open for contrast. This piece was worked in three pieces: the center front, left side, and right side. The two sidepieces were attached using the pleat method as well.

Materials

3 tubes 8° hex beads*

3 tubes 11° Japanese seed beads*

1 tube 10° triangles in complementary colors

1 tube round Czech seed beads

6 to 9 bronze irradiated freshwater pearls

Nylon beading thread

#12 beading needle

Thread conditioner

Scissors

Sectioned ceramic watercolor dish

*Make sure each tube varies from the others in styles and finishes.

Finished size: 19"

Instructions

1. Thread the needle, double the thread, and condition it.

2. Add a tension bead and then thread on 4" of 8° hex beads.

3. Begin to single-peyote stitch these beads by creating a base row. On the second row, do not stitch all the way to the end, stopping one bead short of the end. Stitch back down the row and stop one bead short of the end. Continue stitching back and forth, stopping short of the end bead in each previous row, until you're only stitching about a 2" row.

4. Needle through the bead fabric to the end of the first row you stitched and repeat steps 1 through 3, stopping short of each row. You will create an elongated oval piece of beadwork. Stop stitching at the end of a row.

To create an arch:

1. Thread on enough beads of a new color and size to create an arch that will go from one end of the edge of the beadwork to the other edge.

2. Anchor the arch and begin stitching on that arch, adding an extra bead on the end of each row, until you are stitching a row that is about 5" long.

3. Once the row is 5" long, continue stitching, but stop each row one bead shorter than the row before. When you are down to a 2" row, you should have a piece of beadwork that looks like two elongated ovals attached at the side with a gap between them.

4. Repeat steps 1 through 3 to create a third elongated oval that is 6" long in the center, mixing the beads in this section.

5. Add two more elongated ovals, using a variety of beads to the other side of the 6" oval. When this step is complete, you will have five ovals that are tacked together with long arches between them.

To create the pleated effect:

1. Thread a new needle, double the thread, and condition it.

2. Anchor the thread in the center of one of the ovals.

3. Determine which side of the beadwork you want to be the front, needle over to the top of one of the arches, and bring the needle out the back.

4. Pinch up the edges of two ovals along one of the arches, so the edges are brought forward to the front.

5. Holding the edges so the back of the beadwork is facing up, begin to stitch through the beads to zip the two ovals together, as shown. Do not worry if the ovals are not perfectly aligned, this will add visual interest to the front of the piece.

Step 5

6. Needle over to another arch between two ovals, pinch up the edges near the top of the beadwork, flip the piece over, and begin to zip the arch closed, but stop zipping when you are two-thirds of the way down the opening.

7. Flip the beadwork back over and examine your progress. Do you like what you see? Needle over and begin to zip another arch closed, but add a pearl or some other bead to the fabric so the pearl appears to be peeking through from the back.

8. Continue adding ovals with big arches between them until you have created the front portion of the necklace that pleases you. Vary the sizes of the pleats and how far you zip them closed.

To create the side pieces:

1. Determine how long you want this necklace to be when completed. By holding the beadwork up to your neck, gauge how long the two side pieces will need to be to go around your neck and clasp in the back. It will probably require an 8" or 9" length, to have extra length for overlapping and attaching to the front piece.

2. Start a new piece of beadwork by threading the needle, doubling the thread, and conditioning it.

3. Thread on 9" of beads, adding them in groups of about 1".

4. Begin to peyote stitch up and down the piece, as shown, adding arches as you go. Periodically, hold the sidepiece next to the front to gauge the proportion. When it is nearly wide enough, set this piece aside.

5. Repeat steps 2 through 4 four the other side of the necklace.

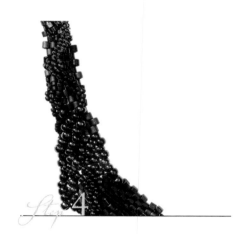

To attach the sides to the center:

1. Arrange the three pieces on your work surface. Determine which of the two sidepieces will be the left and which will be the right.

2. Thread your needle, double the thread, and condition it.

3. Do not anchor the thread! You will be basting (temporarily stitching together) the sidepieces onto your front piece to test how you want to attach them together by zipping them together with one row of stitching.

4. Fit the right side and front piece together and lightly baste the two together. You can overlap the edges and just stitch down through the beadwork for now.

5. Repeat steps 2 through 4 for the other side.

6. Hold the necklace up and fit it around your neck. How does it feel? Are the side pieces long enough? (Remember, we will be adding the beaded toggle clasp, so you will have an opportunity to make the side pieces a little longer.) Make some notes on what you need to do from a construction point of view.

7. Pull out the basting thread from one side and anchor the thread in the beadwork.

8. Attach each sidepiece to the front by zipping the sides to the front piece, for a finished look like that shown below.

To create the beaded clasp:

1. The bar portion of the clasp should be stitched onto the left side of the project. Needle through to the end of the sidepiece and add nine 11° beads.

2. Single-peyote stitch back along these nine beads and when you get to the center, add another nine beads and stitch back to the center. Continue stitching back and forth along these beads to create a toggle for the necklace.

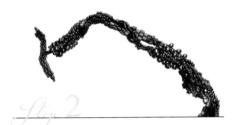

In step 2 of the beaded clasp section, you will want to fill the beads of the clasp bar with as much thread as you can, pulling the thread tightly so the beadwork is quite stiff. Needle through the beads that anchor the toggle as well to reinforce that section.

3. At the other end of the necklace, securely anchor a thread and string on 2½" of beads and stitch back using peyote stitch.

4. Bend the strip around to create a loop. Test the loop to see if it is large enough. (You can always make the loop smaller, but it's challenging to have to cut a loop of several rows of beads to enlarge it!) Anchor the loop by attaching to the beadwork.

5. Once you're satisfied with the length of the loop, stitch back and forth on the loop to increase the width. You will want to stitch back and forth through the beads on the loop to reinforce the beadwork and to fill the beads with as much thread as possible. This section takes a lot of wear and tear when worn.

Meteoric Shards Necklace

This necklace combines the three primary techniques showcased in this book: wirework, stringing, and improvisational beadwork. I created the antiqued silver pieces on this necklace with Precious Metal Clay. You could duplicate the pieces and use silver polymer clay that is antiqued with black acrylic paint for a similar effect.

Materials

20 10mm to 12mm lampwork beads
(Note: the hole must be able to slide onto the wire diameter.)

3 decorative metal or polymer clay pieces (Pieces should have several holes to stitch through in order to attach to the beadwork. Carved jade or other semiprecious stones can be substituted as well.)

4 to 6 oz. metallic and matte finish beads: size 8° hex beads and size 11° Japanese seed beads in purple shades, silver, and black

4 to 6 oz. matte bugle beads

2 to 3 oz. matte purple "E" beads

2 to 3 oz. silver metallic round Czech seed beads

36" 14-gauge silver coated copper wire

6 36" lengths .019 metal core stringing cord

Silver clasp with three loops

6 silver crimp beads

Thread conditioner

Nylon beading thread

#12 beading needle

Scissors

Wire cutters

Round nose pliers

Needle nose pliers

Crimping pliers

Sectioned ceramic watercolor dish

Flat file

Clear tape (optional)

Finished size: 22"

Instructions

1. Reserving 10 lampwork beads for the strap portion of the necklace, cut the wire and file the end.

2. Slide the remaining 10 lampwork beads onto the wire and put a loop onto the end of the wire, as detailed on page 35.

3. File the other end of the wire, put a loop on that end, slide a bead up to that loop, and begin looping and shaping the wire to form the foundation for the beadwork—the wirework base. When the bending is complete, the two wire loops must end up at the upper left and right corners of the front section of the necklace, as these loops are where the sides of the necklace will connect.

In step 3, be sure to position the beads so they do not all fall in a clump. Use the round nose pliers to help bend the loops. In this project, the wire is very curvy, "swervy," and loopy. There are no right angles at all.

4. Thread the needle, double the thread, and condition it.

5. Add a tension bead, slide on 4" of 8º hex beads, and then begin to single-peyote stitch these beads by creating a base row.

6. On the second row, do not stitch all the way to the end, stopping one bead short of the end. Stitch back down the row and stop one bead short of the other end. Continue stitching back and forth in this manner, stopping short of the end bead in each previous row, until you're only stitching about a 2" row.

7. Needle through the beading to the end of the first row you stitched and repeat steps 4 through 6, using a new bead and stopping short of each row. You will create an elongated oval piece of beadwork. Stop stitching at the end of a row. Do not cut off the thread

8. Start a new thread, double it, and condition it.

9. Slide on 4" of the small silver metallic seed beads. Begin peyote stitching, adding an extra bead on the end of each row, until you are stitching a row that is about 5" long.

10. Once the row is 5" long, continue stitching, but stop each row one bead shorter than the row before. When you are down to a 2" row, you should have a piece of beadwork that looks like an elongated oval. Do not cut off the thread.

11. Overlap the narrow ends of the two pieces and stitch them together by zipping up a small section of the edges.

12. Repeat steps 4 through 7 to create more beaded ovals, varying the beads used as well as the length of the swatch.

To attach beadwork to the left side of the necklace:

Notice how the upper edges of the beadwork on the left are attached at the top.

1. The goal is to loosely drape the first beadwork piece so it flows across the necklace front. Add another piece and allow to overlap and curve in and out of the wirework base. Add five to six seed beads to your needle.

2. Drape the beadwork against the wirework base and wrap the thread with the beads around a wire, creating a bead loop.

3. Insert the needle into the stitched beads from the back to anchor the loop.

4. Needle through the stitched beads to go back through the bead loop to reinforce it.

5. Arrange the stitched beads on the wirework base and needle down to a spot where you can add another bead loop.

6. Slide on five to six seed beads to attach the stitched beads to the wirework. Reinforce the loop.

7. Hold one of the metal pieces against the wirework and attach to the wirework base with another bead loop. Reinforce the loop.

To attach beadwork to the center of the necklace:

1. Create another 6"-long elongated oval of stitched beads in another bead color.

2. Create yet another oval using bugle beads.

3. Drape these pieces on the wirework base and attach with bead loops.

4. Stitch them together where needed for support and cohesiveness.

5. Attach another metal piece, using bead loops, so the metal piece is exposed.

To attach beadwork to the right side of the necklace:

1. Create a large (5" to 6" long) elongated oval with black beads and a small one (2" to 3" long) with silver 11° seed beads.

2. Attach the third metal piece.

3. Create another large elongated oval with the silver seed beads and a small one with the large purple "E" beads.

4. Arrange and attach these ovals to the wirework base with bead loops, capturing the metal piece under one of the elongated ovals.

To add the straps:

1. Insert one length of stringing cord through the left loop on the wirework base and slide on 1" of small seed beads. Repeat with two more lengths.

2. Bring the ends together to double the lengths and slide on a lampwork bead over all six ends, making sure that the seed beads are centered on the stringing cord. There are six stringing lengths coming through the lampwork bead.

3. Add 1" of another bead style to each of the stringing lengths, followed by another lampwork bead, 1" bugle beads, and another lampwork bead. Repeat this two more times until five lampwork beads have been added.

4. Divide the six stringing cords into three groups of two cords.

5. Slide 1" of large-hole seed beads onto one grouping of two cords.

6. Add a crimp bead and thread cords through the loop on one side of the clasp. Insert the cords back through the crimp and through the seed beads. Tug on the end of the cords to tighten and crush the crimp bead with the crimping pliers. Repeat for the other sets of two cords.

7. Repeat steps 1 through 6 for the right strap.

Step 6

Redside Designs Cuff

This cuff has an interesting treatment of the clasp. The darker metallic seed beads pick up the swirling colors of the Redside beads, which are primarily light-colored. The seed beads selected for this project are very subtle in colors, allowing the shape and finish of the beads to create much of the visual interest.

Materials

6 lampwork beads, preferably a coordinated set

8 to 10 oz. size 8° Japanese seed beads, including hexes and rounds in bronze, black, iridescent copper, matte bronze, and burgundy

8 to 10 oz. size 11° Japanese seed beads, including hexes and rounds in bronze, black, iridescent copper, matte bronze, and burgundy

4 to 6 oz. size 11° round seed beads in complementary colors and finishes

2 to 4 oz. gold bugle beads

Bar portion of toggle clasp

24" gold-filled 18-gauge wire

Black Nymo "B" thread

#12 beading needle

Thread conditioner

Scissors

Wire cutters

Round nose pliers

Crimping pliers

Flat file

Ceramic watercolor dish

Finished size: 20"

Instructions

To create the wire base:

1. Working off of the spool, cut off the tip of the wire and file the end.

2. Put a loop on one end of the wire, as described on page 35, and then add a wiggle, as on page 41.

3. Slide a lampwork bead onto the wire and add another wiggle.

4. Continue bending the wire to create a segment about 2½" long.

5. Cut the wire segment off of the spool, file the end, and put a loop on the end.

6. Continue to bend several wire segments, adding lampwork beads along the way, making sure the lampwork beads are not always in the same spot on the segment. Each segment should have a loop on each end.

7. Using the loops, join the segments together to create a bracelet that would reach around your wrist with about ½" extra length.

8. On the end segment, bend the wire to create the toggle bar.

9. On the other end, use round nose pliers to make a small loop.

To make the stitched beadwork:

1. Add a tension bead to the thread, as instructed on page 78.

2. Add enough seed beads to cover the length of the wire framework. Vary the types and colors of the beads along the length of the first row.

3. Peyote stitch back and forth on this row, adding three rows.

4. After stitching the fourth row, begin to attach the beadwork to the wire by weaving through the beadwork. Stitch back and forth on the beadwork, building up the width and integrating the wire framework into the bracelet so the wire and beadwork appear to flow together. Use the small wire loop on the end of the wire to anchor the beadwork.

You will be creating a beaded loop later for the clasp.

5. At one end, stitch back and forth on the beadwork to widen the area.

6. Bend the widened end around the wire framework at the base of the toggle bar and stitch the section closed, zipping the two sides together. Stitch around the base of the toggle bar, decreasing the diameter in the ring if you need to make the beadwork fit closer to the toggle bar. Refer to the decreasing peyote stitch instructions on page 88, if necessary.

7. When you get to the base of the bar, add several beads, using brick stitch and 11° Japanese seed beads (see brick stitch in Chapter 6).

8. Needle back through the base row of brick stitch and add beads to the other side, so that the strip of beads is two or three beads longer than the width of the toggle bar. Stitch back and forth on this row in brick stitch until the strip of beads will wrap around the bar and can be joined to the base row to enclose the toggle bar.

9. When you've added enough width, stitch the end of the beadwork to the base row. Add extra beads where necessary to fill in any gaps in the beadwork.

10. Stitch back and forth through the beads on the toggle bar to reinforce the beadwork and to fill the beads with as much thread as possible. This section will have a lot of wear and tear when worn, as the loop will slip over these beads again and again.

11. At the other end of the necklace, securely anchor a thread and add a beaded loop.

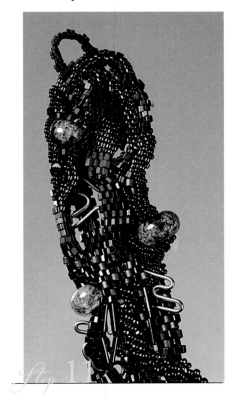

To prevent a gap between the ends of the cuff when worn:

1. Put the loop over the toggle bar.

2. Go to the end where the loop is anchored and begin to stitch back and forth to extend the beadwork (creating a flap) that will cover most of the gap left by the loop. Do not attach this flap to the loop, or you won't be able to close the finding.

3. Reinforce this section to stiffen it and be sure to integrate it into the beadwork by adding texture.

Variations

Option 1: This Redside Beaded Bracelet in Silver uses the same beads as the cuff, but the wire framework is created using 16-gauge sterling silver wire. The wire framework is exposed much more in this project than in the cuff project, with decorative elements in the wire given as much focal attention as the lampwork beads.

The beadwork really consists of purples and blues, and the clasp is formed from the wire. The heavy

16-gauge is quite sturdy for bending into the toggle-style clasp. Bend the wire first and add the beads directly to the wire. You may need the bead reamer to slightly enlarge the holes in the beads so the wire passes through easily. Do not force the beads onto the wire, as this may make them crack with the stress.

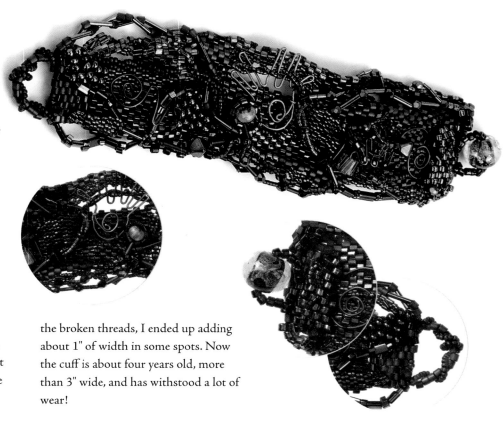

Option 2: This Sculptural Cuff was created soon after I took a class from Jeanette Cook at one of the very first Embellishment shows sponsored by *Bead and Button Magazine*. While the class was on an entirely different subject, Jeanette had brought many samples of her work, as well as her books on sculptural peyote for the students to view.

The cuff features a niobium wire hand and spiral, along with dichroic and furnace glass beads. The clasp is a lampwork bead and a beaded loop.

When I originally created the cuff, it was not as wide as is it is in the photo. After wearing it for about a year, I caught one of the loops on something and broke the threads. In the process of repairing

the broken threads, I ended up adding about 1" of width in some spots. Now the cuff is about four years old, more than 3" wide, and has withstood a lot of wear!

Fringed Fantasia Amulet Bag Necklace

The personal challenge I gave myself when creating this piece was to make each fringe using a different technique and not repeating any one method. The body of the bag started out as a strip of beadwork.

Materials

4 to 6 oz. size 8° hex beads in assorted colors

5 to 7 oz. size 8° Japanese seed beads in assorted colors

8 to 10 oz. size 11° gold Delicas

20 oz. two styles Japanese bugle beads in assorted colors

4 to 6 oz. seed beads in several sizes

Focal bead

10 to 15 special beads: freshwater pearls, miracle beads, crystals, faceted round beads, and faceted teardrop beads

Nymo "B" thread

10" 22-gauge Niobium wire

#12 beading needle

Thread conditioner

Scissors

Wire cutters

Round nose pliers

Crimping pliers

Sectioned ceramic watercolor dish

Finished size: 3" x 5" bag with 22" strap

Instructions

1. Thread a needle, double the thread, and condition.

2. String on 54 assorted 8° beads (or enough beads to create the diameter bag you want) in groups of four to seven of each color or texture.

3. Stitch in basic peyote, matching the base row beads for the first three rows.

4. Once you have three or four rows with 8° beads, begin varying the bead sizes in the stitch. As you add beads of varying sizes, it may help to think of the 8° beads as a single unit and two 11° beads as one unit. Try to create patches of color and texture as you add beads, and be sure to try to blend the patches into one another.

To create an arch:

1. Pass through a bead, add six beads, skip three beads, pass through the next raised bead, and continue as before, adding beads to complete the round.

2. When you stitch your way back to the arch, add beads to the bead arch in the same manner as the peyote stitch.

Add as many gaps as you wish and vary the length of the openings. Consider adding a larger bead and then adding an arch over it. You can add more than one arch in a row, but be sure that you don't add so many arches that the beadwork loses its shape. You'll need to reinforce the arches to give them strength. Be sure to scatter pearls, faceted beads throughout the beadwork as you stitch to create visual texture and interest.

To embellish:

1. Bend a wire hand out of the niobium wire, as instructed on page 43.

2. Stitch the wire hand onto the center of the beadwork, using bead loops.

3. Continue beading back and forth on the project.

4. Add an arch around the end of the wire hand and build up the arch with two or three rows.

5. Use seed bead loops to attach the fingers to the arch to reinforce the beadwork.

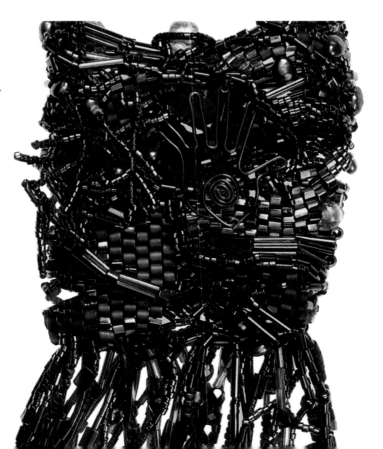

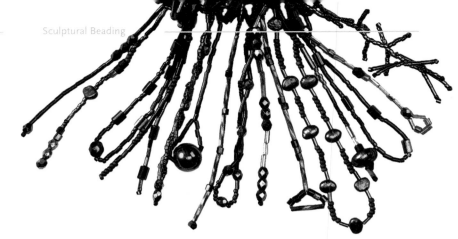

To create the bag:

1. When you have a piece of beadwork that is about 7" long and at least 3" high, stitch until your needle is at the end of a row.

2. Fold the ends of the beadwork toward the middle and overlap one end over the other slightly. You may need to try each end in front to determine which end you prefer.

3. Needle through the beadwork to attach the two ends together to create a tube. Keep in mind that you don't have to perfectly align the ends. Stitch through the back of the beadwork that will be in the front to anchor it. Some of the visual interest in this project will be created by the texture on the end that's in front. It will look like a ruffle.

4. Stitch back and forth on the end that's in front. Add some larger beads or charms.

5. Position a focal bead in the top of the crevice formed by bringing the two ends to the middle and stitch through it to anchor it to the beadwork. Continue building the upper edge of the tube.

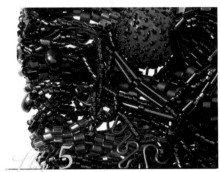

To close the bottom:

1. Continue adding rounds until the bag is the size you desire and decide which side of the bag will become the front.

2. Add three rows of flat peyote to the front using 8° beads and stitching back and forth on the edge that is the front when you compress the sides of the beadwork together.

3. Fold up this flap and fit the staggered beads into the beads of the bag back. Add another row, if necessary, so the beads easily interlock.

4. Stitch the bottom and bag back together, zipping the two portions together, and adding beads (as necessary) to fill any gaps.

5. Anchor the thread in the beadwork to end.

To add the fringe:

1. Thread a needle with a new thread, double the thread, and condition it.

2. Anchor the thread in the bead fabric and bring the needle out at the bag front's bottom left side.

3. Thread on 2" of assorted seed beads, ending with a special bead.

4. Add a pivot bead and pass back through the special bead and up through the beads on the fringe.

5. Finish fringe strand by putting a half-hitch over the threads where you anchor the fringe.

6. Continue adding a variety of fringe strands using different techniques until the bottom of the bag is completely embellished.

To finish:

1. Find the center of one of the upper edges of the bag and begin to stitch in flat peyote stitch to create a narrow strap that is three beads wide.

2. Continue stitching back and forth on the strap until it is the length you desire.

3. Anchor the strap to the other side by zipping it onto the side of the bag.

4. Add additional textural embellishment up the sides and onto the strap in order to integrate the strap into the beadwork, stitching up the strap for several inches.

Black and White and Red All Over Necklace

This 19" necklace features Ellie Mac focal beads, with the secondary beads from Kennebunkport Bead Art. The combination of red, white, and black is a popular design choice, and these beads are really fun. Through the addition of arches and bridges, the feeling of movement was created. The sterling silver slide clasp worked well with the peyote-stitched beadwork, as it helps the beadwork to appear as a continuing band.

Gallery

Fringe Necklace with Skeleton Key

While experimenting in the studio one night, lampwork artist Kim Ballor tried creating a bead right on the skeleton key and loved how it turned out. Thus, this finished 24" piece with its lampwork beads, skeleton key, and seed beads.

Spiny Knotted Necklace

In this 20" necklace, Stephanie Sersich used a technique she developed for when linen and threads are used to bind beads together. Stephanie says that one of the things she enjoys most is working her lampwork beads into unique and complementary combinations. Her inspiration was drawn from the organic elements found all around us.

Abalone Freeform Necklace

Freeform peyote allows Louise Duhamel's necklace to dictate its own flow around three beautiful pieces of Abalone shell. Each section is beaded individually and then they are joined with delicate strands of seed beads, glass, and pearls that bring the necklace together while keeping the focal points center stage.

Fall Splendor

This impressive 31" x 11½" piece was created by Wendy Ellsworth in 2000, using seed beads in freeform peyote and tubular herringbone stitches.

Earth Fire

This Wendy Ellsworth piece was created in 2000, using freeform gourd stitch and features a large Australian opal coupled with glass seed beads, a dichroic button, lampworked beads, and other miscellaneous beads. It is 21½" x 6" x 3¾".

Collage Necklace III

"Exquisite and delicate" are the words Diane Fitzgerald likes to use when describing this 21" necklace. It is made with metal leaves, pearls, pressed glass beads, and seed beads.

Tiger Hill Dragon Necklace

On a trip to China, designer Nancy Hoerner saw a play at Tiger Hill Park in which several men wore a long dragon costume and attacked a tiger. This 22" necklace—finely crafted with a cloisonné charm, glass beads, pottery shards, seashell fragments, and seed beads—represents that dragon.

St. Francis Necklace

Finding an antique bracelet with the clasp and several links intact inspired Nancy Hoerner to create this 24" piece. The pictures on the links reminded her of St. Francis, thus the name, and she chose green glass beads and seed beads to go with this theme.

Resources

Lampwork Bead Artists

Kim Ballor
Kim Ballor Beads
Plymouth, Michigan
www.kimballor.com

Kennebunkport Beads
Kennebunkport, Maine
www.kportbeadart.com

Sylvie Elise Lansdowne
Sylviebeads
Roswell, Georgia
www.sylviebeads.com

Kristan Childs & Julio Wray
Redside Designs
Eugene, Oregon
www.redsidedesigns.net

Paula Radke
Paula Radke Dichroics
Morrow Bay, California
Phone: (800) 341-4945
www.paularadke.com

Stephanie Sersich
Portland, Maine
www.sssbeads.com

Barbara Becker Simon
Cape Coral, Florida
www.bbsimon.com

Vendors

Many of the supplies and tools can be found at your local bead store, craft store, or in larger chain stores, such as Michaels, A.C. Moore, Hobby Lobby, and JoAnn's.

Artistic Wire, Ltd.
Elmhurst, Illinois
Phone: (630) 530-7567
www.artisticwire.com

Beadalon
West Chester, Pennsylvania
Phone: (866) 4BEADALON
www.beadalon.com

Beadbabe.com
Sacramento, California
Phone: (800) 270-4181
www.beadbabe.com

Beads Galore
Tempe, Arizona
Phone: (480) 921-3949
www.beadsgalore.com

Beadniks
Vineyard Haven, Massachusetts
Phone: (866) 861-2323
www.beadgoeson.com

Beyond Beadery
Rollinsville, Colorado
Phone: (800) 840-5548
www.beyondbeadery.com

Caravan Beads
Portland, Maine
Phone: (800) 230-8941
www.caravanbeads.com

Halcraft USA Inc.
New York, New York
Phone: (800) 725-2723
www.halcraft.com

HHH Enterprises
Abilene, Texas
Phone: (800) 777-0218
www.hhhenterprises.com

Knot Just Beads
Wauwatosa, Wisconsin
Phone: (414) 771-8360
www.knotjustbeads.com

PMC Connection
Dallas, Texas
Phone: (866) PMC-CLAY
www.pmcconnection.com

Rio Grande
Albuquerque, New Mexico
Phone: (800) 545-6566
www.riogrande.com

Soft Flex Company
Sonoma, California
Phone: (707) 938-3539
www.softflexcompany.com

WigJig
Arlington, Virginia
Phone: (800) 579-WIRE
www.wigjig.com

Periodicals

Bead Unique Magazine
www.allamericancrafts.com
Publisher: All American Crafts
(Newton, New Jersey)

Beadwork Magazine
www.interweave.com
Publisher: Interweave Press
(Loveland, Colorado)

Bead & Button Magazine
www.beadandbutton.com
Publisher: Kalmbach Publications
(Brookfield, Wisconsin)
Also publishes: *Art Jewelry Magazine*
and *Bead Style Magazine*

Ornament Magazine
Phone: (800) 888-8950
Publisher: Ornament Inc.
(San Marcos, California)

Lapidary Journal
www.lapidaryjournal.com
Publisher: Primedia Inc.
(Devon, Pennsylvania)
Also Publishes: *Colored Stone,*
Step-by-Step Beads

Wire Artist Magazine
www.wag.on.ca
Publisher: The Wire Artists Group
(Stratford, Ontario, Canada)

*B*ibliography

Clegg, Helen, and Mary Larom. *Making Wire Jewelry: 60 Easy Projects in Silver, Copper and Brass.* Asheville, North Carolina. Lark Books, 1997.

Conner, Wendy Simpson. *The Best Little Beading Book, Techniques and More: A Practical Guide for Bead Lovers.* La Mesa, California. Interstellar Trading & Publishing Company, 1995.

Cook, Jeanette, and Vicki Star. *Beading with Peyote Stitch.* Loveland, Colorado. Interweave Press Inc., 2000.

Davis, Jane. *The Complete Guide to Beading Techniques.* Iola, Wisconsin. Krause Publications, Inc., 2001

Gourley, Elizabeth, and Ellen Talbott. *Quick and Easy Beaded Jewelry.* Iola, Wisconsin. Krause Publications, Inc., 2002.

Lareau, Mark. *All Wired Up: Wire Techniques for the Beadworker and Jewelry Maker.* Loveland, Colorado. Interweave Press Inc., 2000.

McGuire, Barbara. *Wire in Design: Modern Wire Art and Mixed Media.* Iola, Wisconsin. Krause Publications Inc., 2001.

Root, Gineke. *Innovative Beaded Jewellry Techniques.* Sydney, Australia. Kangaroo Press Pty Ltd., 1994.

Wells, Carol Wilcox. *Creative Bead Weaving.* Asheville, North Carolina. Lark Books, 1996.

Wells, Carol Wilcox. *The Art and Elegance of Beadweaving: New Jewelry Designs with Classic Stitches.* New York, New York. Sterling Publishing Company, Inc., 2003.

Contributing Artists

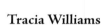

Kim Ballor
Kim Ballor Beads
Plymouth, Michigan
www.kimballor.com

Bonnie Clewans
The Bead Gallery
Amherst, New York
www.beadgallery.com

Louise Duhamel
Belle Melange
Carlsbad, California
www.louiseduhamel.com

Wendy Ellsworth
Quakertown, Pennsylvania
www.ellsworthstudios.com

Diane Fitzgerald
Beautiful Beads
Minneapolis, Minnesota
www.dianefitzgerald.com

Connie Fox
Jatayu
San Diego, California
www.conniefox.com

Marla Gassner
San Diego California
MGas726@cs.com

Nancy Hoerner
St. Paul, Minnesota

Kate McKinnon
Modern Nymph
St. Louis, Missouri
www.modernnymph.com

Stephanie Sersich
Portland, Maine
www.sssbeads.com

Tracia Williams
Tracia & Company Inc.
Orlando, Florida

About the Author

Lynda Musante has been making and selling jewelry for more than 10 years. Musante has published many articles and three books on jewelry-making, teaches jewelry-making, and also works with craft industry manufacturers to develop and market their products. In 2002, Musante began working in altered art and co-authored a book with seven colleagues—a wild group of women affectionately self-titled "Art's Angels."

Currently living in Lawrence, Kansas, with her husband and two children, Musante enjoys teaching others to look at their work in new ways and exploring new skills and techniques. She teaches beading and Precious Metal Clay classes at the University of Richmond and the Lynchburg Fine Arts Center. Musante has appeared on *The Carol Duvall Show* (HGTV) and *Home Matters* (Discovery) to demonstrate jewelry techniques.

EXPLORE
Endless Possibilities

WITH BEADS

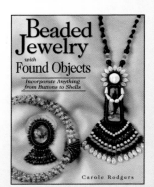

Beaded Jewelry with Found Objects
Incorporate Anything from Buttons to Shells
by Carole Rodgers

Match designer jewelry-reflective of your impeccable taste-with each outfit you own! Details more than 30 original projects using items that can be found in hardware stores, fishing tackle stores, flea markets, glass items, game pieces, cabochons, and other natural objects. Projects, such as the Amethyst Crystal Necklace-made with a pie-shaped slice of amethyst crystal on a chain of amethyst and lavender seed beads, are photographed and accompanied by clear instructions. Basic skills, such as making neck straps, are also explained with detailed, step-by-step instructions.

Softcover • 8-1/4 x 10-7/8 • 128 pages
100+ color photos, plus illus.
Item# BJFO • $19.99

The Art & Soul of Glass Beads
by Susan Ray & Richard Pearce

Take a one-on-one journey with twelve exceptional glass bead artists and learn the origins and renaissance of lampwork glass beads and how to create more than 20 new projects. Follow the step-by-step instructions and beautiful photography to easily create stunning necklaces, earrings, bracelets, and much more. Discover the serendipity of the artists' creative process, including how to choose color and materials, and how to add the finishing touches.

Softcover • 8-1/4 x 10-7/8 • 144 pages
250 color photos
Item# GLABD • $24.99

Decorative Wirework
by Jane Davis

You'll find fresh, new and exciting ideas for working with wire in this new book from author Jane Davis. Create more than 50 projects, including earrings, brooches, bracelets, window treatments and candleholders with her easy-to-follow instructions, detailed illustrations and beautiful photographs. Projects are appropriate for all skill levels.

Softcover • 8-1/4 x 10-7/8 • 128 pages
100+ color photos, 100+ illus.
Item# DCWK • $19.95

Quick & Easy Beaded Jewelry
by Elizabeth Gourley and Ellen Talbott

You'll find hours of fun and inspiration for making your own unique and fashionable beaded jewelry in this new book! Includes 30 lovely projects for making matching necklaces, bracelets, earrings, and rings using beading techniques such as stranding, peyote stitching, and netting. Detailed directions, lavish photography, and illustrations guide you through each project quickly and easily.

Softcover • 8-1/4 x 10-7/8 • 128 pages
75 color photos
Item# QEBJ • $19.95

The Complete Guide to Beading Techniques
30 Decorative Projects
by Jane Davis

This is the most complete volume of beading techniques on the market, filled with gorgeous photos of antique and contemporary beadwork that will inspire beaders of any skill level. After learning about the basic terms and tools, you will explore each technique, including beadweaving, crochet, and tambourwork, and complete a sampler to reinforce the skill learned. Finally, 30 elegant projects, such as table settings, Christmas ornaments, lampshades, a purse, and pincushion, ranging in difficulty from beginner to expert, are included.

Softcover • 8-1/4 x 10-7/8 • 160 pages
100 illus. • 150 color photos
Item# BEHME • $24.95

A Beader's Reference
by Jane Davis

Feel inspired to create beautiful beaded masterpieces with this new reference offering a multitude of patterns for motifs and centerpieces, borders and cords, and fringes and edgings. The hundreds of easy-to-follow beading graphs and how-to illustrations can be your secret to looking like an accomplished beading professional. With three pattern sections, a project section with instructions for 12 projects, and a contributing artists' gallery, this book provides more inspiration for creating beautiful beaded pieces than any other of its kind.

Softcover • 8-1/4 x 10-7/8 • 160 pages
300+ charts & illus. • 100 color photos
Item# BDREF • $24.99